WHAT'S YOUR MARK?
EVERY MOMENT COUNTS.

ZONDERVAN®

LOOK INSIDE **YOURSELF**. EVERY MOMENT COUNTS.

WHAT'S YOUR MARK?

JEREMY COWART - CURATION AND PHOTOGRAPHY

ANNIE F. DOWNS - INTERVIEWS AND WRITTEN CONTENT

BRAD DAVIS - LAYOUT AND DESIGN

MICHAEL MOORE - PRODUCER

———————————

JOIN THE MOVEMENT

SHARE
YOUR
MARK.COM

———————————

THE BOOK OF MARK

INTERVIEWS

FROM THE PUBLISHER

I am a publisher, a follower of Christ and a creative. As a publisher I find inspiration from what people do, not what they say. As a follower of Christ, I publish unique works of Scripture that help more people absorb God's Word more often. And as a creative, I get energized by people who use their gifts to make a mark in the world. Jeremy Cowart's work in both his professional and his personal life should open your eyes to the vast possibilities for making your own mark.

Jeremy began making his mark globally in 2005 when he photographed Africa's AIDS generation, helping to document the hope and pain of these children and families. In 2008, Jeremy founded Help-Portrait, a global community of photographers giving back to people in need. In 2010, Jeremy brought art supplies to communities in Haiti so they could express their feelings about the devastation in Port-au-Prince from the earthquake. Just one year later, Jeremy traveled to Rwanda to document genocide survivors who live harmoniously among the killers of their families. Most recently, the art therapy that Jeremy provided child soldiers in Uganda made a mark on the world. It is impossible to list all of the ways Jeremy has been a devoted servant of God. It is, however, easy to understand why I am honored to bring you Jeremy's work embedded in the Gospel of Mark.

As a publisher, a follower of Christ and a creative, I am humbled to work side by side with Jeremy Cowart as he continues to make his mark on the world. He has influenced me and I know he will influence you. With newfound inspiration, I ask you, *What's Your Mark?*

Chip Brown, Senior Vice President and Publisher

FOREWORD BY
JEREMY COWART

This book isn't meant merely to be consumed. It's meant to be digested. This isn't a book to celebrate the best in others as much as it is a book meant to call out the best in you.

We're on this journey together, noticing the passions in others that have changed this globe because of the Man who changed each of them: Jesus Christ. He is the ultimate mark on our planet, the ultimate mark on countless lives, and his hands and feet display the ultimate marks of sacrifice.

Each of the mark-makers featured in this book, from the superstars to the heroes to the everyday folks, have been marked by Christ and, in turn, they have marked the world. To spoil the ending, here is the truth: it doesn't matter who you are, how big your audience or your bank account, you can make a mark.

Have you? Do you want to? Are you just waiting for someone to say, "You can do it"?

You can do it. These people did. Jesus did. He is the example, the eternal Truth we love because he loved us first. We serve because he served first.

Hold this book near as you set out on your own world-marking adventure. As you identify that thing that only you can do, remind yourself of these faces, these stories, and know that your life matters. You are making a difference.

Every moment counts. Let's prove it.

Want to see what others are doing to make their mark? Check out **SHAREYOURMARK.COM**

CLAIRE DIAZ-ORTIZ

TWITTER FOR GOOD

CLAIRE DIAZ-ORTIZ
TWITTER FOR GOOD

Because of the digital revolution that is going on all around us, we are each leaving marks that, for generations to come, will be searchable, google-able and viewable. No one is more aware of the need to make a positive impact in that world than Claire Diaz-Ortiz. Author of Twitter for Good: Change the World One Tweet at a Time and a senior executive at Twitter, Claire spends her days encouraging Twitter users to use the medium to help, to give and to connect.

Long before she was a top-ranking member of the Twitter staff, Claire joined the 140-character networking site while staying in an orphanage in Kenya as one of her last stops on a trip around the world in 2009. Claire was moved to stay on at the orphanage, doing whatever she could to help the orphans. And she used Twitter as a way to spread the news about the good work that the orphanage was accomplishing. Claire's use of Twitter was also a way to connect with others interested in helping orphans and working to collect resources for the work. The orphanage was making a mark, and others needed to hear about it. Claire has since begun a nonprofit organization, Hope Runs, that benefits AIDS orphans in the same region.

Passionate about development and education, Claire works to train and equip Twitter users, particularly churches, church leaders and nonprofit organizations, who are eager to connect with their audiences.

TWITTER FOR GOOD CONTINUED ON NEXT PAGE

CLAIRE DIAZ-ORTIZ
TWITTER FOR GOOD CONTINUED

"When someone begins on Twitter, I tell them one thing: Ask yourself, 'Who can I help?'" Claire can teach others this truth because she lives this truth.

Claire holds an MBA from Oxford University, where she was a Skoll Foundation Scholar for Social Entrepreneurship. She also has a BA and MA in anthropology from Stanford University. With over 300,000 followers, many of whom she connects with and responds to, Claire is also a blogger, author and international speaker while maintaining her role of leading social innovation at Twitter. Reading her feed, one can see that she cares about connecting with her followers, educating them and helping others—she is making a mark, in her own way, on the social media world.

Unlike other social media outlets, Twitter is built to intrinsically help users make a mark. "Twitter is about creating and cultivating new relationships," Claire says. "We should always be thinking about how to widen our nets." Whether it is replying to a celebrity or meeting others who have similar interests in a Twitter chat, you are capable, every time you write those 140 characters, to affect those who follow you.

WHAT'S YOUR MARK?

HOW ARE YOU USING SOCIAL MEDIA TO MAKE A POSITIVE MARK ON THE WORLD?

Claire's foster son, Sammy, whom she met while living in the orphanage in Kenya, recently graduated from high school in the US and is now serving in Ecuador with the Global Citizen Year program before returning to the US for college.
Photo credit: "Sammy Ikna" by Jillian West

"THE TIME HAS COME," HE SAID. "THE KINGDOM OF GOD HAS COME NEAR. REPENT AND BELIEVE THE GOOD NEWS!"

MARK 1:15

John the Baptist Prepares the Way

1 The beginning of the good news about Jesus the Messiah,^{a} the Son of God,^{b} ^{2}as it is written in Isaiah the prophet:

"I will send my messenger ahead of you,
  who will prepare your way"^{c}—
^{3}"a voice of one calling in the wilderness,
  'Prepare the way for the Lord,
  make straight paths for him.' "^{d}

^{4}And so John the Baptist appeared in the wilderness, preaching a baptism of repentance for the forgiveness of sins. ^{5}The whole Judean countryside and all the people of Jerusalem went out to him. Confessing their sins, they were baptized by him in the Jordan River. ^{6}John wore clothing made of camel's hair, with a leather belt around his waist, and he ate locusts and wild honey. ^{7}And this was his message: "After me comes the one more powerful than I, the straps of whose sandals I am not worthy to stoop down and untie. ^{8}I baptize you with^e water, but he will baptize you with^e the Holy Spirit."

The Baptism and Testing of Jesus

^{9}At that time Jesus came from Nazareth in Galilee and was baptized by John in the Jordan. ^{10}Just as Jesus was coming up out of the water, he saw heaven being torn open and the Spirit descending on him like a dove. ^{11}And a voice came from heaven: "You are my Son, whom I love; with you I am well pleased."

^{12}At once the Spirit sent him out into the wilderness, ^{13}and he was in the wilderness forty days, being tempted^f by Satan. He was with the wild animals, and angels attended him.

Jesus Announces the Good News

^{14}After John was put in prison, Jesus went into Galilee, proclaiming the good news of God. ^{15}"The time has come," he said. "The kingdom of God has come near. Repent and believe the good news!"

Jesus Calls His First Disciples

^{16}As Jesus walked beside the Sea of Galilee, he saw Simon and his brother Andrew casting a net into the lake, for they were fishermen. ^{17}"Come, follow me," Jesus said, "and I will send you out to fish for people." ^{18}At once they left their nets and followed him.

^{19}When he had gone a little farther, he saw James son of Zebedee and his brother John in a boat, preparing their nets. ^{20}Without delay he called them, and they left their father Zebedee in the boat with the hired men and followed him.

> When someone begins on Twitter, I tell them one thing: Ask yourself, "Who can I help?"
>
> **CLAIRE DIAZ-ORTIZ**

Jesus Drives Out an Impure Spirit

^{21}They went to Capernaum, and when the Sabbath came, Jesus went into the synagogue and began to teach. ^{22}The people were amazed at his teaching, because he taught them as one who had authority, not as the teachers of the law. ^{23}Just then a man in their synagogue who was possessed by an impure spirit cried out, ^{24}"What do you want with us, Jesus of Nazareth? Have you come to destroy us? I know who you are—the Holy One of God!"

^{25}"Be quiet!" said Jesus sternly. "Come out of him!" ^{26}The impure spirit shook the man violently and came out of him with a shriek.

^{27}The people were all so amazed that they asked each other, "What is this? A new teaching—and with authority! He even gives orders to impure spirits and they obey him." ²⁸News about him spread quickly over the whole region of Galilee.

Jesus Heals Many

²⁹As soon as they left the synagogue, they went with James and John to the home of Simon and Andrew. ³⁰Simon's mother-in-law was in bed with a fever, and they immediately told Jesus about her. ³¹So he went to her, took her hand and helped her up. The fever left her and she began to wait on them.

³²That evening after sunset the people brought to Jesus all the sick and demon-possessed. ³³The whole town gathered at the door, ³⁴and Jesus healed many who had various diseases. He also drove out many demons, but he would not let the demons speak because they knew who he was.

Jesus Prays in a Solitary Place

³⁵Very early in the morning, while it was still dark, Jesus got up, left the house and went off to a solitary place, where he prayed. ³⁶Simon and his companions went to look for him, ³⁷and when they found him, they exclaimed: "Everyone is looking for you!"

³⁸Jesus replied, "Let us go somewhere else—to the nearby villages—so I can preach there also. That is why I have come." ³⁹So he traveled throughout Galilee, preaching in their synagogues and driving out demons.

Jesus Heals a Man With Leprosy

⁴⁰A man with leprosyᵍ came to him and begged him on his knees, "If you are willing, you can make me clean."

> It's about others, seeing the light in them, focusing on who they are, and remembering that it isn't your circumstance that defines you.
>
> **ESTHER HAVENS**

⁴¹Jesus was indignant.ᵇ He reached out his hand and touched the man. "I am willing," he said. "Be clean!" ⁴²Immediately the leprosy left him and he was cleansed.

⁴³Jesus sent him away at once with a strong warning: ⁴⁴"See that you don't tell this to anyone. But go, show yourself to the priest and offer the sacrifices that Moses commanded for your cleansing, as a testimony to them." ⁴⁵Instead he went out and began to talk freely, spreading the news. As a result, Jesus could no longer enter a town openly but stayed outside in lonely places. Yet the people still came to him from everywhere.

Jesus Forgives and Heals a Paralyzed Man

2 A few days later, when Jesus again entered Capernaum, the people heard that he had come home. ²They gathered in such large numbers that there was no room left, not even outside the door, and he preached the word to them. ³Some men came, bringing to him a paralyzed man, carried by four of them. ⁴Since they could not get him to Jesus because of the crowd, they made an opening in the roof above Jesus by digging through it and then lowered the mat the man was lying on. ⁵When Jesus saw their faith, he said to the paralyzed man, "Son, your sins are forgiven."

⁶Now some teachers of the law were sitting there, thinking to themselves, ⁷"Why does this fellow talk like that? He's blaspheming! Who can forgive sins but God alone?"

⁸Immediately Jesus knew in his spirit that this was what they were thinking in their hearts, and he said to them, "Why are you thinking these things? ⁹Which is easier: to say to this paralyzed man, 'Your

ESTHER HAVENS

LOOK PAST YOURSELF

ESTHER HAVENS
LOOK PAST YOURSELF

Photographers spend their lives looking at others. Humanitarian photographer Esther Havens believes this is the key to being the kind of human who makes a mark: Look past yourself; see other people.

Esther began her journey to making a mark as a photographer while traveling with the nonprofit organization Youth With A Mission to India in the spring of 2002. God used that time on the mission field to show her how valuable she was to him. She had to first love herself, and only then was her capacity to love others increased. She learned to see others as Christ sees them.

After that trip, Esther knew she wanted to pursue photography to help others. Using her camera, Esther captures moments where the light shines on the subjects in such a way that God's light is reflected. She bridges that gap between the person in the picture and the person looking at the picture, and she walks alongside communities and organizations to record those light-filled moments.

Esther sees her work as connecting with the subject of the photograph and connecting with the viewer of the picture. Photographers have the unique opportunity, Esther says, to gain

LOOK PAST YOURSELF CONTINUED ON NEXT PAGE

ESTHER HAVENS
LOOK PAST YOURSELF CONTINUED

the trust of the those involved with the making of the art. To stand in front of them, look into their eyes and their lives, and see them as human. Because of her unique style and inspiring images, she has worked on social-awareness campaigns with organizations such as Charity: Water, TOMS Shoes, Concern Worldwide and Warby Parker.

It's about others, seeing the light in them, focusing on who they are, and remembering that it isn't your circumstance that defines you. Esther is making a mark by not looking at herself at all. "You aren't doing this for yourself," Esther says with a pause in her voice, "God uses us for others—to treat people with dignity, love them unconditionally and help change lives."

WHAT'S YOUR MARK?

HOW CAN YOU LOOK PAST YOURSELF TO MAKE A MARK ON OTHERS?

In 2008, the only water available to Manwoondi was from this muddy hole. This village now has clean water.
Photo credit: "Manwoondi" by Esther Havens Photography

"IT IS NOT THE HEALTHY WHO NEED A DOCTOR, BUT THE SICK. I HAVE NOT COME TO CALL THE RIGHTEOUS, BUT SINNERS."

MARK 2:17

LECRAE

HONEST WORDS

LECRAE

HONEST WORDS

He could say what we want to hear. But Lecrae can't live like that. His convictions won't allow it. That's not making a mark; that's covering your mark to make sure it doesn't cause any raised eyebrows. Lecrae is a Christian hip-hop artist signed to Reach Records, the record label that he cofounded. He is a loud voice in Christian culture, especially in urban communities. But he sees the flaws in the Christian culture and the hip-hop culture at large. Through his music and life, he seeks to paint a more accurate picture of church and of Jesus.

"A Christian culture has been developed," he says, "that isn't inviting. It is honesty and transparency that people relate to—whether you are talking about pain or joy. Jesus wanted the low, the prostitutes and tax collectors and the sinners, to feel comfortable around him, but he was always honest. I want to be like that—I want to be a hospital, not an exclusive hotel."

Lecrae's passion for others plays out not only in his music but also in his nonprofit, ReachLife Ministries. ReachLife equips leaders in urban communities with resources to help them help others. With conferences, curriculum, books and music, leaders throughout the United States are encouraged and supported to live honestly, lead openly, and inspire and equip students to make a mark of their own.

HONEST WORDS CONTINUED ON NEXT PAGE

LECRAE

HONEST WORDS CONTINUED

The recipient of many nominations and awards, including a Grammy nomination for "Best Rap/ Rock album" in 2010 and a Dove Award for "Rap/Hip Hop Recorded Song of the Year and Rap/ Hip Hop Album of the Year" in 2012, Lecrae is displaying for all that what draws ears to your words, what makes a mark, is telling the truth in a beautifully gritty or hauntingly poetic form. His most recent album, *Gravity*, released in the fall of 2012, speaks of the weight of this world, the challenges we all face. Not one to sugarcoat situations, the rawness of Lecrae's lyrics mixed with the heart-thumping beats of this album will call out honesty in the listener. Lecrae makes a mark with his music far more profound than we could ever judge.

"Know that you were meant to make a mark," Lecrae says, "and it's that truth, it's those honest words, that will change your everything."

WHAT'S YOUR MARK?

WHAT ARE YOU SAYING THAT IS MAKING A MARK?

Lecrae's shows are energetic, upbeat and inspirational.
Photo credit: "Lecrae Live" by Brody Harper

JESUS WENT UP ON
A MOUNTAINSIDE AND
CALLED TO HIM THOSE
HE WANTED, AND THEY
CAME TO HIM.
HE APPOINTED TWELVE
THAT THEY MIGHT BE
WITH HIM AND THAT HE
MIGHT SEND THEM OUT
TO PREACH.

———————

MARK 3:13-14

sins are forgiven,' or to say, 'Get up, take your mat and walk'? [10]But I want you to know that the Son of Man has authority on earth to forgive sins." So he said to the man, [11]"I tell you, get up, take your mat and go home." [12]He got up, took his mat and walked out in full view of them all. This amazed everyone and they praised God, saying, "We have never seen anything like this!"

Jesus Calls Levi and Eats With Sinners

[13]Once again Jesus went out beside the lake. A large crowd came to him, and he began to teach them. [14]As he walked along, he saw Levi son of Alphaeus sitting at the tax collector's booth. "Follow me," Jesus told him, and Levi got up and followed him.

[15]While Jesus was having dinner at Levi's house, many tax collectors and sinners were eating with him and his disciples, for there were many who followed him. [16]When the teachers of the law who were Pharisees saw him eating with the sinners and tax collectors, they asked his disciples: "Why does he eat with tax collectors and sinners?"

[17]On hearing this, Jesus said to them, "It is not the healthy who need a doctor, but the sick. I have not come to call the righteous, but sinners."

Jesus Questioned About Fasting

[18]Now John's disciples and the Pharisees were fasting. Some people came and asked Jesus, "How is it that John's disciples and the disciples of the Pharisees are fasting, but yours are not?"

[19]Jesus answered, "How can the guests of the bridegroom fast while he is with them? They cannot, so long as they have him with them. [20]But the time will come when the bridegroom will be taken from them, and on that day they will fast.

[21]"No one sews a patch of unshrunk cloth on an old garment. Otherwise, the new piece will pull away from the old, making the tear worse. [22]And no one pours new wine into old wineskins. Otherwise, the wine will burst the skins, and both the wine and the wineskins will be ruined. No, they pour new wine into new wineskins."

Jesus Is Lord of the Sabbath

[23]One Sabbath Jesus was going through the grainfields, and as his disciples walked along, they began to pick some heads of grain. [24]The Pharisees said to him, "Look, why are they doing what is unlawful on the Sabbath?"

[25]He answered, "Have you never read what David did when he and his companions were hungry and in need? [26]In the days of Abiathar the high priest, he entered the house of God and ate the consecrated bread, which is lawful only for priests to eat. And he also gave some to his companions."

[27]Then he said to them, "The Sabbath was made for man, not man for the Sabbath. [28]So the Son of Man is Lord even of the Sabbath."

Jesus Heals on the Sabbath

3 Another time Jesus went into the synagogue, and a man with a shriveled hand was there. [2]Some of them were looking for a reason to accuse Jesus, so they watched him closely to see if he would heal him on the Sabbath. [3]Jesus said to the man with the shriveled hand, "Stand up in front of everyone."

[4]Then Jesus asked them, "Which is lawful on the Sabbath: to do good or to do evil, to save life or to kill?" But they remained silent.

[5]He looked around at them in anger and, deeply distressed at their stubborn hearts, said to the man, "Stretch out your hand." He stretched it out, and his hand was completely restored. [6]Then the Pharisees went out and began to plot with the Herodians how they might kill Jesus.

Crowds Follow Jesus

[7]Jesus withdrew with his disciples to the lake, and a large crowd from Galilee followed. [8]When they

heard about all he was doing, many people came to him from Judea, Jerusalem, Idumea, and the regions across the Jordan and around Tyre and Sidon. ⁹Because of the crowd he told his disciples to have a small boat ready for him, to keep the people from crowding him. ¹⁰For he had healed many, so that those with diseases were pushing forward to touch him. ¹¹Whenever the impure spirits saw him, they fell down before him and cried out, "You are the Son of God." ¹²But he gave them strict orders not to tell others about him.

Jesus Appoints the Twelve

¹³Jesus went up on a mountainside and called to him those he wanted, and they came to him. ¹⁴He appointed twelve*ᵃ* that they might be with him and that he might send them out to preach ¹⁵and to have authority to drive out demons. ¹⁶These are the twelve he appointed: Simon (to whom he gave the name Peter), ¹⁷James son of Zebedee and his brother John (to them he gave the name Boanerges, which means "sons of thunder"), ¹⁸Andrew, Philip, Bartholomew, Matthew, Thomas, James son of Alphaeus, Thaddaeus, Simon the Zealot ¹⁹and Judas Iscariot, who betrayed him.

Jesus Accused by His Family and by Teachers of the Law

²⁰Then Jesus entered a house, and again a crowd gathered, so that he and his disciples were not even able to eat. ²¹When his family*ᵇ* heard about this, they went to take charge of him, for they said, "He is out of his mind."

²²And the teachers of the law who came down

> Know that you were meant to make a mark, and it's that truth, it's those honest words, that will change your everything.
>
> **LECRAE**

from Jerusalem said, "He is possessed by Beelzebul! By the prince of demons he is driving out demons."

²³So Jesus called them over to him and began to speak to them in parables: "How can Satan drive out Satan? ²⁴If a kingdom is divided against itself, that kingdom cannot stand. ²⁵If a house is divided against itself, that house cannot stand. ²⁶And if Satan opposes himself and is divided, he cannot stand; his end has come. ²⁷In fact, no one can enter a strong man's house without first tying him up. Then he can plunder the strong man's house. ²⁸Truly I tell you, people can be forgiven all their sins and every slander they utter, ²⁹but whoever blasphemes against the Holy Spirit will never be forgiven; they are guilty of an eternal sin."

³⁰He said this because they were saying, "He has an impure spirit."

³¹Then Jesus' mother and brothers arrived. Standing outside, they sent someone in to call him. ³²A crowd was sitting around him, and they told him, "Your mother and brothers are outside looking for you."

³³"Who are my mother and my brothers?" he asked.

³⁴Then he looked at those seated in a circle around him and said, "Here are my mother and my brothers! ³⁵Whoever does God's will is my brother and sister and mother."

The Parable of the Sower

4 Again Jesus began to teach by the lake. The crowd that gathered around him was so large that he got into a boat and sat in it out on the lake, while all the people were along the shore at the water's edge. ²He taught them many things by parables,

MARK BURNETT
& ROMA DOWNEY

TAKE A RISK & THE DIVINE AT WORK

MARK BURNETT
TAKE A RISK

Mark Burnett is a talented producer of television shows. He's best known for his work on *Survivor*, *The Apprentice*, *The Voice*, *Shark Tank*, *The People's Choice Awards* and the syndicated hit *Are You Smarter Than a 5th Grader?* "I've tried to do family-friendly programming," he says, "programming that was commercially attractive to a massive audience and thought provoking." Mark's work reaches millions of viewers many nights each week.

"All that matters in television, films and plays is that the story's good. No matter the intent, if the stories aren't good, no one is going to watch," he says. Recently, Mark has set his sights on telling another story, an old story in a new way, making another mark by creatively showing Jesus to the world.

Mark and his wife, actress Roma Downey, produced the ten-hour docudrama *The Bible* for the History Channel. As a kid, Mark was captivated by the special-effects miracles in the film *The Ten Commandments*. Now Mark wants to give viewers a similar experience and use his gifts to create a legacy project, the kind that can touch people around the world. History Channel President Nancy Dubuc says about the project, "For a new generation, Mark and Roma's series provides a way to visit the work in a visual and entertaining way that may encourage viewers to seek more information about the Bible."

TAKE A RISK CONTINUED ON NEXT PAGE

MARK BURNETT
TAKE A RISK CONTINUED

Mark's faith and his ability to tell stories that impact many hearts have left a permanent mark on individuals and our culture. And everyone, he says, whether through an art medium or in their everyday life, can make a mark on our world. "You just have to turn that fear of putting yourself out there into excitement and energy. You have to be willing to take risks, to look stupid and possibly fail. Take that feeling of fear in your stomach—that is the exact same feeling as excitement—and change your perception of what that feeling means."

As Mark has taken risks and continues to do so, his mark on our culture and our world continues to expand.

WHAT'S YOUR MARK?

HOW WILL YOU LET THE LIGHT OF CHRIST SHINE IN YOUR LIFE TO LEAVE A MARK?

History Channel's *The Bible,* produced by Burnett and Downey and starring Downey as Mary the mother of Jesus, beautifully retells many of the most moving Bible stories in epic fashion.
Photo credit: Photo by Joe Albias. © Lightworks Media. All Rights Reserved.

"DO YOU BRING IN A LAMP TO PUT IT UNDER A BOWL OR A BED? INSTEAD, DON'T YOU PUT IT ON ITS STAND?"

MARK 4:21

ROMA DOWNEY
THE DIVINE AT WORK

Roma Downey, an actress and producer, was born and raised in Northern Ireland and has appeared on Broadway and in countless television movies. She is best known for her portrayal of the angel Monica on the hit television show *Touched by an Angel*. The series ran for almost ten years and at the height of its popularity was watched by over 20 million people on a weekly basis. "The central theme was: 'There is a God; God loves you; and God wants to be part of your life," Roma says. "[Playing the part of] the angel, I got to deliver that message every week. As a believer, that was a beautiful privilege."

Roma made a mark through T*ouched by an Ange*l that continues to this day. Through TV syndication, miraculous stories still pour in on how God speaks to hearts through episodes. "There are countless stories of the healing power of love, people hearing for the first time that God wants to be a part of their life. It's a TV show, but it's very powerful to see the Holy Spirit touch people's lives," says Roma. "Playing Monica called on the best parts of myself and deepened my faith; it was a blessing to me as well."

Today Roma is still making a mark, touching others with her life, her art and her stories. She is now at the helm of a new project that has tremendous potential for global impact. She says, "People are hungry for stories that inspire and give hope." So along with her husband, Mark Burnett, Roma has spent over three years working on a ten-hour docudrama for the History Channel entitled *The Bible*. "It is beautiful and exciting. Compelling. Touching. Inspiring. Dramatic. We are breathing fresh visual

ROMA DOWNEY
THE DIVINE AT WORK CONTINUED

life into the sacred and wonderful stories of the Bible," Roma explains. This production will reach people all over the world, people who may never pick up a Bible, may not be able to read or have access to one, but who will turn on the television.

Also, as an ambassador for Operation Smile, Roma sees how the divine is at work through the hands of medical professionals healing children and bringing light into the world.

Roma's faith and her desire to see God at work are what inspire her on to make a mark, to pursue projects like *The Bible* and continue her work with Operation Smile. These things will bring glory to God. "We are all leaving an imprint emotionally, spiritually and physically—and with that comes a great responsibility. We must have courage to leave a mark, to be a part of what God is doing here on Earth."

WHAT'S YOUR MARK?

WHERE DO YOU ALREADY SEE THE DIVINE AT WORK IN YOUR LIFE?

History Channel's *The Bible,* produced by Burnett and Downey and starring Downey as Mary the mother of Jesus, beautifully retells many of the most moving Bible stories in epic fashion.
Photo credit: Photo by Joe Albias. © Lightworks Media. All Rights Reserved.

and in his teaching said: [3]"Listen! A farmer went out to sow his seed. [4]As he was scattering the seed, some fell along the path, and the birds came and ate it up. [5]Some fell on rocky places, where it did not have much soil. It sprang up quickly, because the soil was shallow. [6]But when the sun came up, the plants were scorched, and they withered because they had no root. [7]Other seed fell among thorns, which grew up and choked the plants, so that they did not bear grain. [8]Still other seed fell on good soil. It came up, grew and produced a crop, some multiplying thirty, some sixty, some a hundred times."

[9]Then Jesus said, "Whoever has ears to hear, let them hear."

[10]When he was alone, the Twelve and the others around him asked him about the parables. [11]He told them, "The secret of the kingdom of God has been given to you. But to those on the outside everything is said in parables [12]so that,

> "'they may be ever seeing
>   but never perceiving,
>   and ever hearing but never
>   understanding;
> otherwise they might turn and be forgiven!'[a]"

[13]Then Jesus said to them, "Don't you understand this parable? How then will you understand any parable? [14]The farmer sows the word. [15]Some people are like seed along the path, where the word is sown. As soon as they hear it, Satan comes and takes away the word that was sown in them. [16]Others, like seed sown on rocky places, hear the word and at once receive it with joy. [17]But since they have no root, they last only a short time. When trouble or persecution comes because of the word, they quickly fall away. [18]Still others, like seed sown among thorns, hear the

word; [19]but the worries of this life, the deceitfulness of wealth and the desires for other things come in and choke the word, making it unfruitful. [20]Others, like seed sown on good soil, hear the word, accept it, and produce a crop—some thirty, some sixty, some a hundred times what was sown."

A Lamp on a Stand

[21]He said to them, "Do you bring in a lamp to put it under a bowl or a bed? Instead, don't you put it on its stand? [22]For whatever is hidden is meant to be disclosed, and whatever is concealed is meant to be brought out into the open. [23]If anyone has ears to hear, let them hear."

[24]"Consider carefully what you hear," he continued. "With the measure you use, it will be measured to you—and even more. [25]Whoever has will be given more; whoever does not have, even what they have will be taken from them."

The Parable of the Growing Seed

[26]He also said, "This is what the kingdom of God is like. A man scatters seed on the ground. [27]Night and day, whether he sleeps or gets up, the seed sprouts and grows, though he does not know how. [28]All by itself the soil produces grain—first the stalk, then the head, then the full kernel in the head. [29]As soon as the grain is ripe, he puts the sickle to it, because the harvest has come."

The Parable of the Mustard Seed

[30]Again he said, "What shall we say the kingdom of God is like, or what parable shall we use to describe it? [31]It is like a mustard seed, which is the smallest of

> Everyone, whether through an art medium or in their everyday life, can make a mark.
>
> **MARK BURNETT**

all seeds on earth. [32] Yet when planted, it grows and becomes the largest of all garden plants, with such big branches that the birds can perch in its shade."

[33] With many similar parables Jesus spoke the word to them, as much as they could understand. [34] He did not say anything to them without using a parable. But when he was alone with his own disciples, he explained everything.

Jesus Calms the Storm

[35] That day when evening came, he said to his disciples, "Let us go over to the other side." [36] Leaving the crowd behind, they took him along, just as he was, in the boat. There were also other boats with him. [37] A furious squall came up, and the waves broke over the boat, so that it was nearly swamped. [38] Jesus was in the stern, sleeping on a cushion. The disciples woke him and said to him, "Teacher, don't you care if we drown?"

[39] He got up, rebuked the wind and said to the waves, "Quiet! Be still!" Then the wind died down and it was completely calm.

[40] He said to his disciples, "Why are you so afraid? Do you still have no faith?"

[41] They were terrified and asked each other, "Who is this? Even the wind and the waves obey him!"

Jesus Restores a Demon-Possessed Man

5 They went across the lake to the region of the Gerasenes.*a* [2] When Jesus got out of the boat, a man with an impure spirit came from the tombs to meet him. [3] This man lived in the tombs, and no one could bind him anymore, not even with a chain. [4] For he had often been chained hand and foot, but he tore the chains apart and broke the irons on his feet. No one was strong enough to subdue him. [5] Night and day among the tombs and in the hills he would cry out and cut himself with stones.

[6] When he saw Jesus from a distance, he ran and fell on his knees in front of him. [7] He shouted at the top of his voice, "What do you want with me, Jesus, Son of the Most High God? In God's name don't torture me!" [8] For Jesus had said to him, "Come out of this man, you impure spirit!"

[9] Then Jesus asked him, "What is your name?"

"My name is Legion," he replied, "for we are many." [10] And he begged Jesus again and again not to send them out of the area.

[11] A large herd of pigs was feeding on the nearby hillside. [12] The demons begged Jesus, "Send us among the pigs; allow us to go into them." [13] He gave them permission, and the impure spirits came out and went into the pigs. The herd, about two thousand in number, rushed down the steep bank into the lake and were drowned.

[14] Those tending the pigs ran off and reported this in the town and countryside, and the people went out to see what had happened. [15] When they came to Jesus, they saw the man who had been possessed by the legion of demons, sitting there, dressed and in his right mind; and they were afraid. [16] Those who had seen it told the people what had happened to the demon-possessed man — and told about the pigs as well. [17] Then the people began to plead with Jesus to leave their region.

[18] As Jesus was getting into the boat, the man who had been demon-possessed begged to go with him. [19] Jesus did not let him, but said, "Go home to your

> We are all leaving an imprint emotionally, spiritually and physically — and with that comes a great responsibility.
>
> **ROMA DOWNEY**

JEFF SHINABARGER

SOLVING PROBLEMS

JEFF SHINABARGER
SOLVING PROBLEMS

"Our generation wants to do more than tell about problems, they want to solve them." Jeff Shinabarger speaks passionately about the simplicity that we have before us, the ability to see a problem and find a simple solution. Jeff is the founder of GiftCardGiver.com and Plywoodpeople.com and the author of *More or Less: Choosing a Lifestyle of Excessive Generosity.* His life is focused on identifying problems in his community and in our world, and he continues to make a mark by stepping into those situations and offering hope, help and a solution.

Jeff's dad was a pastor. Jeff grew up with a unique view of the social problems and personal struggles in the lives of the congregation and the community. He watched as his father not only came up with solutions but became part of the solutions. A resident of Atlanta, he heads down to the Martin Luther King Jr. Center each year to remember those lessons learned as a child, to help those in need and be a part of the solution. "I can't solve every problem," Jeff says. "I'm part of a bigger story than that—and we all want to be a part of that story, the Gospel story, to build into each other's passions and make community around that."

Jeff believes that one of the greatest ways to make a mark is to equip others to do the same. When he's encouraging people to find their passionate area of service, he says that gaining experience and

SOLVING PROBLEMS CONTINUED ON NEXT PAGE

SOLVING PROBLEMS CONTINUED

knowledge through a wide variety of opportunities will really show what you are passionate about. "It'll all boil down and you have to find that opportunity that is the best for you." Whether it is on a personal family level or on the level of global impact, finding that problem that makes you feel alive to solve is the key to making a mark. "Influence is gained by doing something, not just talking about it."

But Jeff hasn't quit making the rubber meet the road in his own life. "I don't think you should learn from me unless I am in the mess of solving a problem myself." And so he does; he lives like that, finding opportunities to share problems with folks who may be able to help solve them, but also stepping into local community needs himself by doing things as simple as providing a beautifully painted bench for his neighborhood bus stop.

"We all want to be known," he says, "but when we are addressing problems, we become associated with the solution." And that kind of mark won't soon be forgotten.

WHAT'S YOUR MARK?

IS THERE A PROBLEM IN YOUR COMMUNITY THAT YOU CAN HELP SOLVE?

Making a mark on Atlanta is something great leaders have done for years. In the future, people will tell stories of communities that were better off because of Jeff's commitment to this town.
Photo credit: "The City of Freedom" by Ben Farnham

"GO HOME TO YOUR OWN PEOPLE AND TELL THEM HOW MUCH THE LORD HAS DONE FOR YOU."

MARK 5:19

FRED KATAGWA

EDUCATE

FRED KATAGWA

EDUCATE

Since 2002, Fred Katagwa has been the executive director of Africa New Life Ministries Rwanda. For the past ten years, this ministry has stretched across the nation of Rwanda and has served tens of thousands of people. The areas of ministry include child sponsorship, vocational training, providing clean water and operating a health clinic.

As the executive director, Fred oversees the schools run by Africa New Life Ministries. "We strive to leave a mark on the community," Fred says. And it is clear that is happening. The nation's poorest children are being educated at one of the nation's top schools, New Life Christian Academy, run by this ministry.

Fred believes in teaching by way of example, and that starts at the top with him and the headmasters of the schools and funnels down to the teachers and the students. "Many of our students struggle with a 'failure' mentality," he says. "We work to discover the abilities that lie within them and help them overcome that attitude."

Fred has a vision to transform students' lives and leave a permanent mark. "The brain of a child is wet cement," says Fred, "and having them in school is the place where we can leave that mark—as teachers, as administrators." Over 4,000 students are being helped by Africa New Life Ministries in

EDUCATE CONTINUED ON NEXT PAGE

EDUCATE CONTINUED

Rwanda. Whether through providing full tuition for school, mentorship from caring adults or being nourished through a meal program, these children are being cared for and educated.

Others are seeing the excellence with which Fred and his staff lead the schools. The government of Rwanda recently handed over a school for Africa New Life to run, and UNICEF gave a school in the Bugesera district to the ministry to manage. With highly qualified educators, a safe environment and competitive curriculum, it is clear why these schools are ranked at the top in the nation of Rwanda.

Fred is proud of the last ten years of Africa New Life Ministries and looks to the years ahead with great excitement. "We are a pencil in the hand of God," he says. "It's not about us. Our lives speak, our actions speak, far louder than our words." Fred spends his days making a mark by teaching others—from the leadership to the students to his staff. Education has marked him, and his goal is to continue that in the lives of the children of Rwanda.

WHAT'S YOUR MARK?

HOW CAN YOU USE WHAT YOU KNOW TO INSPIRE OTHERS TO MAKE A MARK?

By encouraging educators and administrators throughout their schools, Fred enables students to learn and make a mark with their lives.
Photo credit: "Africa New Life School" by Esther Havens Photography

OVERHEARING WHAT THEY SAID, JESUS TOLD HIM, "DON'T BE AFRAID; JUST BELIEVE."

MARK 5:36

own people and tell them how much the Lord has done for you, and how he has had mercy on you." [20] So the man went away and began to tell in the Decapolis[b] how much Jesus had done for him. And all the people were amazed.

Jesus Raises a Dead Girl and Heals a Sick Woman

[21] When Jesus had again crossed over by boat to the other side of the lake, a large crowd gathered around him while he was by the lake. [22] Then one of the synagogue leaders, named Jairus, came, and when he saw Jesus, he fell at his feet. [23] He pleaded earnestly with him, "My little daughter is dying. Please come and put your hands on her so that she will be healed and live." [24] So Jesus went with him.

A large crowd followed and pressed around him. [25] And a woman was there who had been subject to bleeding for twelve years. [26] She had suffered a great deal under the care of many doctors and had spent all she had, yet instead of getting better she grew worse. [27] When she heard about Jesus, she came up behind him in the crowd and touched his cloak, [28] because she thought, "If I just touch his clothes, I will be healed." [29] Immediately her bleeding stopped and she felt in her body that she was freed from her suffering.

[30] At once Jesus realized that power had gone out from him. He turned around in the crowd and asked, "Who touched my clothes?"

[31] "You see the people crowding against you," his disciples answered, "and yet you can ask, 'Who touched me?'"

[32] But Jesus kept looking around to see who had done it. [33] Then the woman, knowing what had hap-

> One of the greatest ways to make a mark is to equip others to do the same.
>
> **JEFF SHINABARGER**

pened to her, came and fell at his feet and, trembling with fear, told him the whole truth. [34] He said to her, "Daughter, your faith has healed you. Go in peace and be freed from your suffering."

[35] While Jesus was still speaking, some people came from the house of Jairus, the synagogue leader. "Your daughter is dead," they said. "Why bother the teacher anymore?"

[36] Overhearing[c] what they said, Jesus told him, "Don't be afraid; just believe."

[37] He did not let anyone follow him except Peter, James and John the brother of James. [38] When they came to the home of the synagogue leader, Jesus saw a commotion, with people crying and wailing loudly. [39] He went in and said to them, "Why all this commotion and wailing? The child is not dead but asleep." [40] But they laughed at him.

After he put them all out, he took the child's father and mother and the disciples who were with him, and went in where the child was. [41] He took her by the hand and said to her, *"Talitha koum!"* (which means "Little girl, I say to you, get up!"). [42] Immediately the girl stood up and began to walk around (she was twelve years old). At this they were completely astonished. [43] He gave strict orders not to let anyone know about this, and told them to give her something to eat.

A Prophet Without Honor

6 Jesus left there and went to his hometown, accompanied by his disciples. [2] When the Sabbath came, he began to teach in the synagogue, and many who heard him were amazed.

"Where did this man get these things?" they asked.

"What's this wisdom that has been given him? What are these remarkable miracles he is performing? ³Isn't this the carpenter? Isn't this Mary's son and the brother of James, Joseph,ᵃ Judas and Simon? Aren't his sisters here with us?" And they took offense at him.

⁴Jesus said to them, "A prophet is not without honor except in his own town, among his relatives and in his own home." ⁵He could not do any miracles there, except lay his hands on a few sick people and heal them. ⁶He was amazed at their lack of faith.

Jesus Sends Out the Twelve

Then Jesus went around teaching from village to village. ⁷Calling the Twelve to him, he began to send them out two by two and gave them authority over impure spirits.

⁸These were his instructions: "Take nothing for the journey except a staff—no bread, no bag, no money in your belts. ⁹Wear sandals but not an extra shirt. ¹⁰Whenever you enter a house, stay there until you leave that town. ¹¹And if any place will not welcome you or listen to you, leave that place and shake the dust off your feet as a testimony against them."

¹²They went out and preached that people should repent. ¹³They drove out many demons and anointed many sick people with oil and healed them.

John the Baptist Beheaded

¹⁴King Herod heard about this, for Jesus' name had become well known. Some were saying,ᵇ "John the Baptist has been raised from the dead, and that is why miraculous powers are at work in him."

¹⁵Others said, "He is Elijah."

> We strive to leave a mark on the community.
>
> **FRED KATAGWA**

And still others claimed, "He is a prophet, like one of the prophets of long ago."

¹⁶But when Herod heard this, he said, "John, whom I beheaded, has been raised from the dead!"

¹⁷For Herod himself had given orders to have John arrested, and he had him bound and put in prison. He did this because of Herodias, his brother Philip's wife, whom he had married. ¹⁸For John had been saying to Herod, "It is not lawful for you to have your brother's wife." ¹⁹So Herodias nursed a grudge against John and wanted to kill him. But she was not able to, ²⁰because Herod feared John and protected him, knowing him to be a righteous and holy man. When Herod heard John, he was greatly puzzledᶜ; yet he liked to listen to him.

²¹Finally the opportune time came. On his birthday Herod gave a banquet for his high officials and military commanders and the leading men of Galilee. ²²When the daughter ofᵈ Herodias came in and danced, she pleased Herod and his dinner guests.

The king said to the girl, "Ask me for anything you want, and I'll give it to you." ²³And he promised her with an oath, "Whatever you ask I will give you, up to half my kingdom."

²⁴She went out and said to her mother, "What shall I ask for?"

"The head of John the Baptist," she answered.

²⁵At once the girl hurried in to the king with the request: "I want you to give me right now the head of John the Baptist on a platter."

²⁶The king was greatly distressed, but because of his oaths and his dinner guests, he did not want to refuse her. ²⁷So he immediately sent an executioner

GARY HAUGEN

LEAVE

GARY HAUGEN

LEAVE

Gary Haugen believes in "the yearning to catapult," the desire in each of us to make a difference, to launch out into something new. Gary is the president and CEO of International Justice Mission (IJM), a human rights agency that secures justice for victims of slavery, sexual exploitation and other forms of violent oppression.

His own desire to launch out to make a difference propelled him to found IJM and to leave his high-level job as senior trial attorney with the Police Misconduct Task Force of the Civil Rights Division of the US Department of Justice, "I knew I was doing a good thing at the Justice Department. But I also knew that if I left, someone else would be hired to make sure there was justice in the United States," Gary says. "I made a decision to speak for those who were experiencing violent and huge injustices in other parts of the world."

So he left. Gary left a powerful job to rescue the powerless. "If you want your light to burn brightly, take it to the darkest places." And that is what Gary and IJM do daily. He and his staff choose to leave behind comfort and security, rescuing the oppressed every day. Since 2005, IJM has assisted more than 11,000 individuals, many of whom were victims of forced-labor slavery or sex trafficking, provided aftercare for thousands and implemented projects to protect whole communities. And it all took leaving—Gary, the staff, the brave victims who are rescued. Everyone had to leave to make a mark.

LEAVE CONTINUED ON NEXT PAGE

GARY HAUGEN
LEAVE CONTINUED

Even Jesus. Jesus made his mark by leaving heaven for us. "Jesus rescues us so that we can be a part of the larger work of rescue in the world," Gary explains.

Gary has received multiple human rights awards and has been profiled on television shows and in many articles. He feels his leaving was just the next natural step. It wasn't easy, but it was right. "If you want to make a mark," Gary says, "go where people are having the hardest time believing God is good." Leave where you are. Go there.

WHAT'S YOUR MARK?

WHAT CAN YOU LEAVE TO MAKE YOUR MARK?

IJM Kenya staff celebrate with the family of Joseph, an innocent man who was released from prison through IJM's advocacy.
Photo credit: *No title given* by Amy Lucia for © International Justice Mission

"A PROPHET IS NOT WITHOUT HONOR EXCEPT IN HIS OWN TOWN, AMONG HIS RELATIVES AND IN HIS OWN HOME."

MARK 6:4

JENA NARDELLA

BUILD A BRIDGE

JENA NARDELLA
BUILD A BRIDGE

In Zambia they say "*panono panono*," or "brick by brick," as a reminder to focus on the importance of the slow build, the recognition that every step matters. Jena Nardella lives this reality and experiences it every day as the executive director of Blood:Water Mission, a nonprofit organization based in Nashville, Tennessee, established to empower communities to work against the HIV/AIDS and water crises in sub-Saharan Africa through creative grassroots efforts.

Jena was always that girl, the one in high school who got voted "most likely to devote your life to a 'lost cause,'" the one who was always trying to help others, the one who could see a bridge between two communities and wanted to build it, cross it and lead others over it. As a college student, Jena majored in nursing, seeing the profession as a way to help others. After learning more about HIV, how it attacks the weakest points of the weakest members of society, she switched to political studies, hoping to make a larger impact on the HIV crisis in Africa.

When she switched majors, Jena built a bridge that day—a bridge to step out in faith and begin her future career. As a senior in college, Jena met the multi-platinum GRAMMY award-winning band Jars of Clay and heard of their vision and passion for those in Africa in need of water and medical supplies, and she saw a way to partner with them to make a difference. At only 22 years old, she moved to Nashville to cofound and work at Blood:Water and has been there ever since. Now as

BUILD A BRIDGE CONTINUED ON NEXT PAGE

JENA NARDELLA
BUILD A BRIDGE CONTINUED

executive director, it is Jena's job to build bridges between those in need in Africa and those able to help elsewhere. She travels to Africa multiple times a year to connect with communities in need and monitor the projects firsthand. To date, Blood:Water has partnered with more than 1,100 communities in Africa, providing life-saving water for over 700,000 people in 11 different countries and access to HIV/AIDS education, treatment and support for over 30,000 people. Jena also spends her time working to clearly communicate the message of Blood:Water and connect with people passionate to partner with them.

Brick by brick, Jena encourages others to make a mark in everyday opportunities. "Success doesn't always mean a big splash," she says, "but we have to be faithful in the day to day." And so she is. And the bricks she lays every day, and the marks she makes on both sides of the ocean, are building bridges that will last for a long time.

WHAT'S YOUR MARK?

HOW CAN YOU MAKE A MARK BY BUILDING A BRIDGE FOR SOMEONE ELSE?

Blood:Water Mission provides clean water wells for communities across Africa.
Photo credit: "Samiya" by Pamela Crane for Blood:Water Mission

WHEN JESUS LANDED AND SAW A LARGE CROWD, HE HAD COMPASSION ON THEM, BECAUSE THEY WERE LIKE SHEEP WITHOUT A SHEPHERD.

MARK 6:34

with orders to bring John's head. The man went, beheaded John in the prison, [28] and brought back his head on a platter. He presented it to the girl, and she gave it to her mother. [29] On hearing of this, John's disciples came and took his body and laid it in a tomb.

Jesus Feeds the Five Thousand

[30] The apostles gathered around Jesus and reported to him all they had done and taught. [31] Then, because so many people were coming and going that they did not even have a chance to eat, he said to them, "Come with me by yourselves to a quiet place and get some rest."

[32] So they went away by themselves in a boat to a solitary place. [33] But many who saw them leaving recognized them and ran on foot from all the towns and got there ahead of them. [34] When Jesus landed and saw a large crowd, he had compassion on them, because they were like sheep without a shepherd. So he began teaching them many things.

[35] By this time it was late in the day, so his disciples came to him. "This is a remote place," they said, "and it's already very late. [36] Send the people away so that they can go to the surrounding countryside and villages and buy themselves something to eat."

[37] But he answered, "You give them something to eat."

They said to him, "That would take more than half a year's wages[c]! Are we to go and spend that much on bread and give it to them to eat?"

[38] "How many loaves do you have?" he asked. "Go and see."

When they found out, they said, "Five—and two fish."

> To make a mark, go where people are having the hardest time believing God is good.
>
> **GARY HAUGEN**

[39] Then Jesus directed them to have all the people sit down in groups on the green grass. [40] So they sat down in groups of hundreds and fifties. [41] Taking the five loaves and the two fish and looking up to heaven, he gave thanks and broke the loaves. Then he gave them to his disciples to distribute to the people. He also divided the two fish among them all. [42] They all ate and were satisfied, [43] and the disciples picked up twelve basketfuls of broken pieces of bread and fish. [44] The number of the men who had eaten was five thousand.

Jesus Walks on the Water

[45] Immediately Jesus made his disciples get into the boat and go on ahead of him to Bethsaida, while he dismissed the crowd. [46] After leaving them, he went up on a mountainside to pray.

[47] Later that night, the boat was in the middle of the lake, and he was alone on land. [48] He saw the disciples straining at the oars, because the wind was against them. Shortly before dawn he went out to them, walking on the lake. He was about to pass by them, [49] but when they saw him walking on the lake, they thought he was a ghost. They cried out, [50] because they all saw him and were terrified.

Immediately he spoke to them and said, "Take courage! It is I. Don't be afraid." [51] Then he climbed into the boat with them, and the wind died down. They were completely amazed, [52] for they had not understood about the loaves; their hearts were hardened.

[53] When they had crossed over, they landed at Gennesaret and anchored there. [54] As soon as they got out of the boat, people recognized Jesus. [55] They

ran throughout that whole region and carried the sick on mats to wherever they heard he was. ⁵⁶And wherever he went—into villages, towns or countryside—they placed the sick in the marketplaces. They begged him to let them touch even the edge of his cloak, and all who touched it were healed.

That Which Defiles

7 The Pharisees and some of the teachers of the law who had come from Jerusalem gathered around Jesus ²and saw some of his disciples eating food with hands that were defiled, that is, unwashed. ³(The Pharisees and all the Jews do not eat unless they give their hands a ceremonial washing, holding to the tradition of the elders. ⁴When they come from the marketplace they do not eat unless they wash. And they observe many other traditions, such as the washing of cups, pitchers and kettles.ᵃ)

⁵So the Pharisees and teachers of the law asked Jesus, "Why don't your disciples live according to the tradition of the elders instead of eating their food with defiled hands?"

⁶He replied, "Isaiah was right when he prophesied about you hypocrites; as it is written:

"'These people honor me with their lips,
    but their hearts are far from me.
⁷They worship me in vain;
    their teachings are merely human rules.'ᵇ

⁸You have let go of the commands of God and are holding on to human traditions."

⁹And he continued, "You have a fine way of setting aside the commands of God in order to observeᶜ your own traditions! ¹⁰For Moses said, 'Honor your father and mother,'ᵈ and, 'Anyone who curses their father or mother is to be put to death.'ᵉ ¹¹But you say that if anyone declares that what might have been used to help their father or mother is Corban (that is, devoted to God)— ¹²then you no longer let them do anything for their father or mother. ¹³Thus you nullify the word of God by your tradition that you have handed down. And you do many things like that."

¹⁴Again Jesus called the crowd to him and said, "Listen to me, everyone, and understand this. ¹⁵Nothing outside a person can defile them by going into them. Rather, it is what comes out of a person that defiles them." [16]ᶠ

¹⁷After he had left the crowd and entered the house, his disciples asked him about this parable. ¹⁸"Are you so dull?" he asked. "Don't you see that nothing that enters a person from the outside can defile them? ¹⁹For it doesn't go into their heart but into their stomach, and then out of the body." (In saying this, Jesus declared all foods clean.)

²⁰He went on: "What comes out of a person is what defiles them. ²¹For it is from within, out of a person's heart, that evil thoughts come—sexual immorality, theft, murder, ²²adultery, greed, malice, deceit, lewdness, envy, slander, arrogance and folly. ²³All these evils come from inside and defile a person."

Jesus Honors a Syrophoenician Woman's Faith

²⁴Jesus left that place and went to the vicinity of Tyre.ᵍ He entered a house and did not want anyone to know it; yet he could not keep his presence secret. ²⁵In fact, as soon as she heard about him, a woman whose little daughter was possessed by an impure spirit came and fell at his feet. ²⁶The woman was a

> Success doesn't always mean a big splash, but we have to be faithful in the day to day.
>
> **JENA NARDELLA**

LAURA LASKY

LAURA LASKY

ACTIONS SPEAK LOUDER

It's like having matching tattoos. Or scars. No one else understands you better than ones who have stood where you have stood, seen what you've seen, lived what you are dying to leave. Laura Lasky is doing just that by revealing her marks from a painful past in order to make marks that heal in the lives of others. Laura is the founder and director of Solace San Francisco, a ministry to reach those in the human trafficking and sex industry throughout a city that is known for its exploits and opportunities. Delivered from her lifestyle choices and addictions that led her into a life in this industry, Laura is able to do what most cannot: see these people as people, not projects. "[God] makes all things new," she says, "and I am evidence that he works all things together for good."

Laura calls them her family, those who use their bodies for the entertainment of others. She doesn't ask them to clean up or make a proclamation or get any stamp of approval; she just shows them her scars, and they feel safe to talk about their own. Laura brings cupcakes and snacks to dancers in the dressing rooms of any of the 15 strip clubs in San Francisco in order to build relationships and open doors of communication. Laura and those who volunteer with her ministry are welcomed in all the clubs in their town. Working with escorts, homosexuals and the transgender community, Solace SF targets these groups and offers help in a variety of areas: mentoring, education, counseling, medical services and more.

ACTIONS SPEAK LOUDER CONTINUED ON NEXT PAGE

LAURA LASKY

ACTIONS SPEAK LOUDER CONTINUED

Laura is soft-spoken. She's kind and unassuming. But inside of Laura burns a fire to see the marginalized treated with loving-kindness and to love people as they are. "If you love someone, you go to them and you wait. Love is patient."

Actions speak louder than words. "They will know us by our love," she says, gently reminding that words can only go so far. It's the moments, the marks shared and made when standing face to face that display Christ to those who are hurting.

WHAT'S YOUR MARK?

HOW CAN YOU USE YOUR HISTORY TO MAKE A MARK ON SOMEONE ELSE'S FUTURE?

As a simple gesture of love, every week Laura and her team deliver cupcakes to the strip clubs of San Francisco.
Photo credit: Photo by Kim A. Thomas Photography

WHEREVER [JESUS] WENT ... THEY PLACED THE SICK IN THE MARKETPLACES. THEY BEGGED HIM TO LET THEM TOUCH EVEN THE EDGE OF HIS CLOAK, AND ALL WHO TOUCHED IT WERE HEALED.

MARK 6:56

Greek, born in Syrian Phoenicia. She begged Jesus to drive the demon out of her daughter.

[27] "First let the children eat all they want," he told her, "for it is not right to take the children's bread and toss it to the dogs."

[28] "Lord," she replied, "even the dogs under the table eat the children's crumbs."

[29] Then he told her, "For such a reply, you may go; the demon has left your daughter."

[30] She went home and found her child lying on the bed, and the demon gone.

Jesus Heals a Deaf and Mute Man

[31] Then Jesus left the vicinity of Tyre and went through Sidon, down to the Sea of Galilee and into the region of the Decapolis.[b] [32] There some people brought to him a man who was deaf and could hardly talk, and they begged Jesus to place his hand on him.

[33] After he took him aside, away from the crowd, Jesus put his fingers into the man's ears. Then he spit and touched the man's tongue. [34] He looked up to heaven and with a deep sigh said to him, *"Ephphatha!"* (which means "Be opened!"). [35] At this, the man's ears were opened, his tongue was loosened and he began to speak plainly.

[36] Jesus commanded them not to tell anyone. But the more he did so, the more they kept talking about it. [37] People were overwhelmed with amazement. "He has done everything well," they said. "He even makes the deaf hear and the mute speak."

Jesus Feeds the Four Thousand

8 During those days another large crowd gathered. Since they had nothing to eat, Jesus called his disciples to him and said, [2] "I have compassion for these people; they have already been with me three days and have nothing to eat. [3] If I send them home hungry, they will collapse on the way, because some of them have come a long distance."

[4] His disciples answered, "But where in this remote place can anyone get enough bread to feed them?"

[5] "How many loaves do you have?" Jesus asked.

"Seven," they replied.

[6] He told the crowd to sit down on the ground. When he had taken the seven loaves and given thanks, he broke them and gave them to his disciples to distribute to the people, and they did so. [7] They had a few small fish as well; he gave thanks for them also and told the disciples to distribute them. [8] The people ate and were satisfied. Afterward the disciples picked up seven basketfuls of broken pieces that were left over. [9] About four thousand were present. After he had sent them away, [10] he got into the boat with his disciples and went to the region of Dalmanutha.

[11] The Pharisees came and began to question Jesus. To test him, they asked him for a sign from heaven. [12] He sighed deeply and said, "Why does this generation ask for a sign? Truly I tell you, no sign will be given to it." [13] Then he left them, got back into the boat and crossed to the other side.

The Yeast of the Pharisees and Herod

[14] The disciples had forgotten to bring bread, except for one loaf they had with them in the boat. [15] "Be careful," Jesus warned them. "Watch out for the yeast of the Pharisees and that of Herod."

[16] They discussed this with one another and said, "It is because we have no bread."

> If you love someone, you go to them and you wait. Love is patient.
>
> **LAURA LASKY**

[17] Aware of their discussion, Jesus asked them: "Why are you talking about having no bread? Do you still not see or understand? Are your hearts hardened? [18] Do you have eyes but fail to see, and ears but fail to hear? And don't you remember? [19] When I broke the five loaves for the five thousand, how many basketfuls of pieces did you pick up?"

"Twelve," they replied.

[20] "And when I broke the seven loaves for the four thousand, how many basketfuls of pieces did you pick up?"

They answered, "Seven."

[21] He said to them, "Do you still not understand?"

Jesus Heals a Blind Man at Bethsaida

[22] They came to Bethsaida, and some people brought a blind man and begged Jesus to touch him. [23] He took the blind man by the hand and led him outside the village. When he had spit on the man's eyes and put his hands on him, Jesus asked, "Do you see anything?"

[24] He looked up and said, "I see people; they look like trees walking around."

[25] Once more Jesus put his hands on the man's eyes. Then his eyes were opened, his sight was restored, and he saw everything clearly. [26] Jesus sent him home, saying, "Don't even go into[a] the village."

Peter Declares That Jesus Is the Messiah

[27] Jesus and his disciples went on to the villages around Caesarea Philippi. On the way he asked them, "Who do people say I am?"

[28] They replied, "Some say John the Baptist; others say Elijah; and still others, one of the prophets."

[29] "But what about you?" he asked. "Who do you say I am?"

Peter answered, "You are the Messiah."

[30] Jesus warned them not to tell anyone about him.

Jesus Predicts His Death

[31] He then began to teach them that the Son of Man must suffer many things and be rejected by the elders, the chief priests and the teachers of the law, and that he must be killed and after three days rise again. [32] He spoke plainly about this, and Peter took him aside and began to rebuke him.

[33] But when Jesus turned and looked at his disciples, he rebuked Peter. "Get behind me, Satan!" he said. "You do not have in mind the concerns of God, but merely human concerns."

The Way of the Cross

[34] Then he called the crowd to him along with his disciples and said: "Whoever wants to be my disciple must deny themselves and take up their cross and follow me. [35] For whoever wants to save their life[b] will lose it, but whoever loses their life for me and for the gospel will save it. [36] What good is it for someone to gain the whole world, yet forfeit their soul? [37] Or what can anyone give in exchange for their soul? [38] If anyone is ashamed of me and my words in this adulterous and sinful generation, the Son of Man will be ashamed of them when he comes in his Father's glory with the holy angels."

9 And he said to them, "Truly I tell you, some who are standing here will not taste death before they see that the kingdom of God has come with power."

> I saw a problem and wanted to do something about it.
>
> **ELLIE AMBROSE**

Today, I run for...

LINAH OKAPEL

Student in The Nike Dance School
The Hawassa Music Sisters Karen

ellie's Run for afRica™

ELLIE AMBROSE

NEVER TOO YOUNG

ELLIE AMBROSE

NEVER TOO YOUNG

Ellie Ambrose was only ten years old when she decided to make a mark. She never called it that, never set out to be a role model or an award winner (though she is both now), she just simply wanted to help. In 2004, Ellie heard a missionary share about his work in a slum of Nairobi, Kenya, about the need and the desperation of the people there. That day in church, seeing a video that showed Africa as more than the *Lion King* images in her head, Ellie responded in a simple way.

Ellie planned a race. It was a simple 5K, the kind of race she had seen be successful. (She also included family games because, as she says, not all of her friends loved to run.) Her parents and her church got on board, and now, in its eighth year, Ellie's Run for Africa in Nashville, Tennessee, has grown to over 1,000 runners and has raised over $350,000. "As a kid, it felt so much more possible than I think it would to me today," Ellie says. "I saw a problem and wanted to do something about it."

Ellie never intended to be the face of this movement; she never pictured it would have the power and the impact it does. The money raised by the runs helps educate students in Africa, including supporting two primary schools, one vocational school and now one high school in Nairobi. Students who previously were unable to go to school due to distance, lack of uniforms or lack of money are now able to grow and learn, thanks to Ellie's Run for Africa.

NEVER TOO YOUNG CONTINUED ON NEXT PAGE

ELLIE AMBROSE
NEVER TOO YOUNG CONTINUED

It's funny to hear Ellie talk about the race—about how it has changed her more than she ever expected, how the kids in Africa are on her mind every day now, and how her life has followed a path that she didn't make but feels honored to be on. Having now been to Africa five times, to Ellie, making a mark means being purposeful in what you do best. New marks are in her future, as this bright eighteen-year-old heads off to college to study nursing. The world is already a better place because of her and will continue to be so as her mark carries on.

WHAT'S YOUR MARK?

**HOW CAN CHILDREN BE EMPOWERED TO MAKE A MARK IN THE WORLD?
WHAT CAN YOU DO TO ENCOURAGE A CHILD TO FULFILL A DREAM?**

Ellie's Run raises money to provide education and more for students in Africa.
Photo credit: "ERFA Photo" by Christi Nolan

SINCE THEY HAD NOTHING TO EAT, JESUS CALLED HIS DISCIPLES TO HIM AND SAID, "I HAVE COMPASSION FOR THESE PEOPLE."

MARK 8:1 - 2

DAN CATHY

INTENTIONAL LEADERSHIP

DAN CATHY
INTENTIONAL LEADERSHIP

Fast-food restaurants are not typically known for their company culture or their remarkable customer service, but since 1946, Chick-fil-A has been breaking the mold of a "typical fast-food experience." And it is their pleasure to do so.

President and COO Dan Cathy leads that charge now, as his father and Chick-fil-A founder, Truett Cathy, did before him. "I'm focused on 'keeping the main thing the main thing.' My dad has always been focused on great food, great service and hospitality. My responsibility today is to continue that charge while keeping the business financially and culturally healthy."

Making a mark through leadership in a large corporation can be challenging. Dan works in an industry that is fast paced and constantly growing, and he must lead a variety of people nationwide. But the principles that the restaurant chain was built on remain intact, and Dan works tirelessly to keep the company focused on their values. "Chick-fil-A was built on Biblical principles," he says, "and we still operate on those timeless principles today. At the same time, our people represent a wide range of faiths, from all walks of life, and we know that our customers are the same way. We treat everyone with honor, dignity and respect. My personal faith leads me to believe that this is the way Jesus would have us operate, but it's also good business."

In the end, Chick-fil-A is still a fast-food restaurant with delicious hand-breaded chicken, hot waffle fries and fresh squeezed lemonade. But the heart behind the counter, that is what makes the difference

INTENTIONAL LEADERSHIP CONTINUED ON NEXT PAGE

DAN CATHY

DAN CATHY
INTENTIONAL LEADERSHIP CONTINUED

and impacts the customers. "The word *restaurant* comes from a French word that means 'a place of restoration.' So, by definition, our job is also to provide a place of comfort, a place of rest, a place where guests will be treated with the utmost hospitality. The fact that we have embraced this definition to not only define what we do but also how we do it has made a big impact on the communities we serve. I'm very thankful and proud to say that I am a restaurateur, and I care deeply about the experiences our guests have with us six days a week."

Dan relies on God to impact the people he serves. "Each of us has boundless potential to leave a mark because we have the promise of God's divine power at work in and through us. When we take the perspective of living out of his limitless reservoir — not just our finite capacity — it's easier to anticipate the exciting potential of each tomorrow with warm hearts, open arms and eager minds. That's when our lives go from just making a living to having a life worth living!" Dan makes a mark daily as he leads intentionally. His corporate staff, the Chick-fil-A operators and team members nationwide, those involved with the WinShape Foundation, and customers at over 1,600 restaurants in 39 states and Washington, D.C. — they all directly benefit from his passion to make a mark through honoring Christ in the workplace.

WHAT'S YOUR MARK?

HOW CAN CHRIST SHINE THROUGH YOU AS YOU LEAD AT YOUR JOB?

As the COO of Chick-fil-A, Dan's leadership makes a mark on many — his corporate staff, the Chick-fil-A operators and team members nationwide.

"WHOEVER WANTS TO BE
MY DISCIPLE MUST DENY
THEMSELVES AND TAKE
UP THEIR CROSS AND
FOLLOW ME.
FOR WHOEVER WANTS
TO SAVE THEIR LIFE WILL
LOSE IT, BUT WHOEVER
LOSES THEIR LIFE FOR
ME AND FOR THE GOSPEL
WILL SAVE IT."

MARK 8:34-35

The Transfiguration

[2] After six days Jesus took Peter, James and John with him and led them up a high mountain, where they were all alone. There he was transfigured before them. [3] His clothes became dazzling white, whiter than anyone in the world could bleach them. [4] And there appeared before them Elijah and Moses, who were talking with Jesus.

[5] Peter said to Jesus, "Rabbi, it is good for us to be here. Let us put up three shelters—one for you, one for Moses and one for Elijah." [6] (He did not know what to say, they were so frightened.)

[7] Then a cloud appeared and covered them, and a voice came from the cloud: "This is my Son, whom I love. Listen to him!"

[8] Suddenly, when they looked around, they no longer saw anyone with them except Jesus.

[9] As they were coming down the mountain, Jesus gave them orders not to tell anyone what they had seen until the Son of Man had risen from the dead. [10] They kept the matter to themselves, discussing what "rising from the dead" meant.

[11] And they asked him, "Why do the teachers of the law say that Elijah must come first?"

[12] Jesus replied, "To be sure, Elijah does come first, and restores all things. Why then is it written that the Son of Man must suffer much and be rejected? [13] But I tell you, Elijah has come, and they have done to him everything they wished, just as it is written about him."

Jesus Heals a Boy Possessed by an Impure Spirit

[14] When they came to the other disciples, they saw a large crowd around them and the teachers of the law arguing with them. [15] As soon as all the people saw Jesus, they were overwhelmed with wonder and ran to greet him.

[16] "What are you arguing with them about?" he asked.

[17] A man in the crowd answered, "Teacher, I brought you my son, who is possessed by a spirit that has robbed him of speech. [18] Whenever it seizes him, it throws him to the ground. He foams at the mouth, gnashes his teeth and becomes rigid. I asked your disciples to drive out the spirit, but they could not."

[19] "You unbelieving generation," Jesus replied, "how long shall I stay with you? How long shall I put up with you? Bring the boy to me."

[20] So they brought him. When the spirit saw Jesus, it immediately threw the boy into a convulsion. He fell to the ground and rolled around, foaming at the mouth.

[21] Jesus asked the boy's father, "How long has he been like this?"

"From childhood," he answered. [22] "It has often thrown him into fire or water to kill him. But if you can do anything, take pity on us and help us."

[23] "'If you can'?" said Jesus. "Everything is possible for one who believes."

[24] Immediately the boy's father exclaimed, "I do believe; help me overcome my unbelief!"

[25] When Jesus saw that a crowd was running to the scene, he rebuked the impure spirit. "You deaf and mute spirit," he said, "I command you, come out of him and never enter him again."

[26] The spirit shrieked, convulsed him violently and came out. The boy looked so much like a corpse that many said, "He's dead." [27] But Jesus took him by the hand and lifted him to his feet, and he stood up.

> Each of us has boundless potential to leave a mark because we have the promise of God's divine power.
>
> **DAN CATHY**

²⁸ After Jesus had gone indoors, his disciples asked him privately, "Why couldn't we drive it out?"

²⁹ He replied, "This kind can come out only by prayer.ᵃ"

Jesus Predicts His Death a Second Time

³⁰ They left that place and passed through Galilee. Jesus did not want anyone to know where they were, ³¹ because he was teaching his disciples. He said to them, "The Son of Man is going to be delivered into the hands of men. They will kill him, and after three days he will rise." ³² But they did not understand what he meant and were afraid to ask him about it.

³³ They came to Capernaum. When he was in the house, he asked them, "What were you arguing about on the road?" ³⁴ But they kept quiet because on the way they had argued about who was the greatest.

³⁵ Sitting down, Jesus called the Twelve and said, "Anyone who wants to be first must be the very last, and the servant of all."

³⁶ He took a little child whom he placed among them. Taking the child in his arms, he said to them, ³⁷ "Whoever welcomes one of these little children in my name welcomes me; and whoever welcomes me does not welcome me but the one who sent me."

Whoever Is Not Against Us Is for Us

³⁸ "Teacher," said John, "we saw someone driving out demons in your name and we told him to stop, because he was not one of us."

³⁹ "Do not stop him," Jesus said. "For no one who does a miracle in my name can in the next moment say anything bad about me, ⁴⁰ for whoever is not against us is for us. ⁴¹ Truly I tell you, anyone who gives you a cup of water in my name because you belong to the Messiah will certainly not lose their reward.

Causing to Stumble

⁴² "If anyone causes one of these little ones—those who believe in me—to stumble, it would be better for them if a large millstone were hung around their neck and they were thrown into the sea. ⁴³ If your hand causes you to stumble, cut it off. It is better for you to enter life maimed than with two hands to go into hell, where the fire never goes out. [44]ᵇ ⁴⁵ And if your foot causes you to stumble, cut it off. It is better for you to enter life crippled than to have two feet and be thrown into hell. [46]ᶜ ⁴⁷ And if your eye causes you to stumble, pluck it out. It is better for you to enter the kingdom of God with one eye than to have two eyes and be thrown into hell, ⁴⁸ where

> "'the worms that eat them do not die,
>   and the fire is not quenched.'ᵈ

⁴⁹ Everyone will be salted with fire.

⁵⁰ "Salt is good, but if it loses its saltiness, how can you make it salty again? Have salt among yourselves, and be at peace with each other."

Divorce

10 Jesus then left that place and went into the region of Judea and across the Jordan. Again crowds of people came to him, and as was his custom, he taught them.

² Some Pharisees came and tested him by asking, "Is it lawful for a man to divorce his wife?"

³ "What did Moses command you?" he replied.

⁴ They said, "Moses permitted a man to write a certificate of divorce and send her away."

⁵ "It was because your hearts were hard that Moses wrote you this law," Jesus replied. ⁶ "But at the beginning of creation God 'made them male and female.'ᵃ ⁷ 'For this reason a man will leave his father and mother and be united to his wife,ᵇ ⁸ and the two will become one flesh.'ᶜ So they are no longer two, but one flesh. ⁹ Therefore what God has joined together, let no one separate."

¹⁰ When they were in the house again, the disciples asked Jesus about this. ¹¹ He answered, "Anyone who divorces his wife and marries another woman

SHAUN KING

EMPOWER

SHAUN KING
EMPOWER

Making a mark isn't a solo performance. The best marks are made when we work in tandem with others, creating a symphony of life change that will always be louder than just one voice. Shaun King, founder of TwitChange, AHomeinHaiti, and founder and CEO of HopeMob, has found a way to not only make a mark himself but to give others permission to do the same. Beginning with his work in Atlanta, providing school supplies for children and helping local families after floods washed through metro Atlanta in 2009, Shaun saw the value and possibility, long before it was popular, of using social media platforms to call people to action.

"Nothing excites me more than empowering somebody to feel like they are a part of a solution to a problem that is too big or too complex or too scary to solve alone." This is what Shaun has done. HopeMob works by telling individual stories and allowing many people to get involved to solve each separate issue. Thus, people are being helped, and people are getting a chance to help. "People get frozen into inaction," Shaun says. But HopeMob breaks a story down to its simplest form—a human in need—and allows others to step in, big or small, and meet that need.

Shaun has won multiple awards for his acts of service and his ability to unite individual givers for the greater good, including a Mashable award for Most Creative Social Good Campaign (TwitChange)

EMPOWER CONTINUED ON NEXT PAGE

EMPOWER CONTINUED

and MSNBC's The Grio Top 100 History Makers. Like some sort of world-changing Pied Piper, Shaun calls people around the globe to action, and they respond. They each make a mark, collectively changing lives.

"Jesus is all about helping people no one else is helping. What motivates me, every day, is that this is how I can be more like Jesus—helping the hurting and those that others have given up on." And Shaun is helping those who watch him too, those who are looking to make a mark but don't know how. He is changing the world by giving the rest of us permission to help. Right now. "The best day to help somebody was probably yesterday, but the next best day is today."

WHAT'S YOUR MARK?

HOW CAN YOU OPEN UP DOORS FOR OTHER PEOPLE TO MAKE A MARK?

Beautiful Haitian children play and run and laugh beside tents provided by AHomeInHaiti.
Photo credit: "A Home in Haiti" by Benjamin Cole Brown

"ANYONE WHO WANTS TO BE FIRST MUST BE THE VERY LAST, AND THE SERVANT OF ALL."

MARK 9:35

MANNY MARTINEZ

CONNECT

MANNY MARTINEZ
CONNECT

"I just started with this simple prayer that God would keep us humble and connect us with the right people." A simple prayer by a humble man. Manny Martinez has seen God answer this prayer for himself and Hello Somebody over and over again. As he has pressed his mark into the world, others' hands have laid their weight upon it as well.

Hello Somebody, the company cofounded by Manny, strives to provide for those less fortunate by creating and selling unique and stylish apparel and then giving the profits to already established organizations that are doing good work on the ground in needy areas around the world. "We are just temporary storage for the funds that God wants to use," Manny says, and Hello Somebody keeps distributing those funds that are brought in through the sales of their products. They feed children in Rwanda, provide water for families in Guatemala, and help aid tornado victims in Joplin, Missouri, just to name a few places of impact. They care about people and desire that people are treated fairly.

They like this position: connected with established, but maybe lesser known, nonprofit organizations, connected with people in need and connected with celebrities who work as the marketing arm for Hello Somebody and the organizations with whom they are partnered. By befriending and working with influencers such as author Jon Acuff and musician Carlos Whittaker, who have "huge platforms of

---

CONNECT CONTINUED ON NEXT PAGE

MANNY MARTINEZ
CONNECT CONTINUED

integrity," as Manny describes them, Hello Somebody has drawn attention and notice from audiences that they would never find on their own. "We build a relationship with these influencers," Manny says, mentioning his heart to minister not only to people in need around the world but to the artists, musicians and authors who partner with Hello Somebody.

As much as he looks to provide for those less fortunate, and it is how he is making his mark, Manny also focuses on connecting with people in his daily life and with the artists who are partnered with Hello Somebody. It's about building relationships, being with the right people at the right time, recognizing that who is beside you is meant to be there.

To Manny, making a mark means connecting with the right people and loving those people well—whether it is a child in need of a meal, a family in need of clean water or a musician in need of a listening ear.

WHAT'S YOUR MARK?

WHICH PEOPLE IS GOD CONNECTING YOU WITH TO HELP YOU MAKE A MARK?

Hello Somebody helps provide for children in need around the world.
Photo credit: "Street Boys Rwanda" by Esther Havens Photography

"FOR EVEN THE SON OF MAN DID NOT COME TO BE SERVED, **BUT TO SERVE, AND TO GIVE HIS LIFE AS A RANSOM FOR MANY.**"

MARK 10:45

commits adultery against her. [12]And if she divorces her husband and marries another man, she commits adultery."

The Little Children and Jesus

[13]People were bringing little children to Jesus for him to place his hands on them, but the disciples rebuked them. [14]When Jesus saw this, he was indignant. He said to them, "Let the little children come to me, and do not hinder them, for the kingdom of God belongs to such as these. [15]Truly I tell you, anyone who will not receive the kingdom of God like a little child will never enter it." [16]And he took the children in his arms, placed his hands on them and blessed them.

The Rich and the Kingdom of God

[17]As Jesus started on his way, a man ran up to him and fell on his knees before him. "Good teacher," he asked, "what must I do to inherit eternal life?"

[18]"Why do you call me good?" Jesus answered. "No one is good—except God alone. [19]You know the commandments: 'You shall not murder, you shall not commit adultery, you shall not steal, you shall not give false testimony, you shall not defraud, honor your father and mother.'[d]"

[20]"Teacher," he declared, "all these I have kept since I was a boy."

[21]Jesus looked at him and loved him. "One thing you lack," he said. "Go, sell everything you have and give to the poor, and you will have treasure in heaven. Then come, follow me."

[22]At this the man's face fell. He went away sad, because he had great wealth.

[23]Jesus looked around and said to his disciples, "How hard it is for the rich to enter the kingdom of God!"

[24]The disciples were amazed at his words. But Jesus said again, "Children, how hard it is[e] to enter the kingdom of God! [25]It is easier for a camel to go through the eye of a needle than for someone who is rich to enter the kingdom of God."

[26]The disciples were even more amazed, and said to each other, "Who then can be saved?"

[27]Jesus looked at them and said, "With man this is impossible, but not with God; all things are possible with God."

[28]Then Peter spoke up, "We have left everything to follow you!"

[29]"Truly I tell you," Jesus replied, "no one who has left home or brothers or sisters or mother or father or children or fields for me and the gospel [30]will fail to receive a hundred times as much in this present age: homes, brothers, sisters, mothers, children and fields—along with persecutions—and in the age to come eternal life. [31]But many who are first will be last, and the last first."

Jesus Predicts His Death a Third Time

[32]They were on their way up to Jerusalem, with Jesus leading the way, and the disciples were astonished, while those who followed were afraid. Again he took the Twelve aside and told them what was going to happen to him. [33]"We are going up to Jerusalem," he said, "and the Son of Man will be delivered over to the chief priests and the teachers of the law. They will condemn him to death and will hand him over to the Gentiles, [34]who will mock him and spit on him, flog him and kill him. Three days later he will rise."

> The best marks are made when we work in tandem with others, creating a symphony of life change.
>
> **SHAUN KING**

The Request of James and John

[35] Then James and John, the sons of Zebedee, came to him. "Teacher," they said, "we want you to do for us whatever we ask."

[36] "What do you want me to do for you?" he asked.

[37] They replied, "Let one of us sit at your right and the other at your left in your glory."

[38] "You don't know what you are asking," Jesus said. "Can you drink the cup I drink or be baptized with the baptism I am baptized with?"

[39] "We can," they answered.

Jesus said to them, "You will drink the cup I drink and be baptized with the baptism I am baptized with, [40] but to sit at my right or left is not for me to grant. These places belong to those for whom they have been prepared."

[41] When the ten heard about this, they became indignant with James and John. [42] Jesus called them together and said, "You know that those who are regarded as rulers of the Gentiles lord it over them, and their high officials exercise authority over them. [43] Not so with you. Instead, whoever wants to become great among you must be your servant, [44] and whoever wants to be first must be slave of all. [45] For even the Son of Man did not come to be served, but to serve, and to give his life as a ransom for many."

Blind Bartimaeus Receives His Sight

[46] Then they came to Jericho. As Jesus and his disciples, together with a large crowd, were leaving the city, a blind man, Bartimaeus (which means "son of Timaeus"), was sitting by the roadside begging. [47] When he heard that it was Jesus of Nazareth, he began to shout, "Jesus, Son of David, have mercy on me!"

[48] Many rebuked him and told him to be quiet, but he shouted all the more, "Son of David, have mercy on me!"

[49] Jesus stopped and said, "Call him."

So they called to the blind man, "Cheer up! On your feet! He's calling you." [50] Throwing his cloak aside, he jumped to his feet and came to Jesus.

[51] "What do you want me to do for you?" Jesus asked him.

The blind man said, "Rabbi, I want to see."

[52] "Go," said Jesus, "your faith has healed you." Immediately he received his sight and followed Jesus along the road.

Jesus Comes to Jerusalem as King

11 As they approached Jerusalem and came to Bethphage and Bethany at the Mount of Olives, Jesus sent two of his disciples, [2] saying to them, "Go to the village ahead of you, and just as you enter it, you will find a colt tied there, which no one has ever ridden. Untie it and bring it here. [3] If anyone asks you, 'Why are you doing this?' say, 'The Lord needs it and will send it back here shortly.'"

[4] They went and found a colt outside in the street, tied at a doorway. As they untied it, [5] some people standing there asked, "What are you doing, untying that colt?" [6] They answered as Jesus had told them to, and the people let them go. [7] When they brought the colt to Jesus and threw their cloaks over it, he sat on it. [8] Many people spread their cloaks on the road, while others spread branches they had cut in the fields.

> It's about building relationships, being with the right people at the right time, recognizing that who is beside you is meant to be there.
>
> **MANNY MARTINEZ**

DONALD COLLINS

MAKE ART

DONALD COLLINS
MAKE ART

Donald Collins didn't feel like he was making a mark. He was simply sketching, drawing the things that caught his eye. He drew faces, trees, the things in his view that remind him of the image of God.

Donald is homeless and lives on the streets of Houston, Texas. It was there in 2012 where he met Jeremy Cowart at a convention called Catalyst Dallas. It is through their friendship that Donald's art and life were brought to the spotlight, and Donald was reminded that he is, in fact, making a mark.

Donald's earliest memories as a child carry him back to his elementary school experience where he would doodle for hours in class, drawing whatever came to his mind. "I wanted to make art more than anything," he says. Many kids quit making art, quit leaving their creative mark on the world when they begin to grow up. "Everyone is a great artist," says Donald, "until they are about 10 and start judging themselves." Donald was the same; he stopped creating art at the age of 19.

Many years later, after ups and downs that left him homeless, he moved to Houston in 2008. He says God gave him back his art when he moved; his eyes were opened again to the power of art and how art affects people. So Donald began to draw again, starting with faces of other homeless men and trees in the park where he spent most of his time. Since June of 2008, Donald has created more than 18,000 images, most of them electronically stored.

MAKE ART CONTINUED ON NEXT PAGE

DONALD COLLINS
MAKE ART CONTINUED

Donald says everyone can make a mark with art and affect those around them. "Instead of looking for heroes, be one and help other people shine." Donald does that as an artist, making a mark by sketching the faces that pass him by, day after day, and sharing his art. Donald also helps others by donating pieces to nonprofit organizations to help them raise funds for a variety of good causes. "If I can make art, I am happy. If I am happy, I share."

WHAT'S YOUR MARK?

HOW CAN YOU USE YOUR ART TO MAKE A MARK ON THE WORLD?

Don draws constantly, every day, as it is his communion with God.
Photo credit: Drawing by Donald Collins for Love Is Studios

"THEREFORE I TELL YOU, WHATEVER YOU ASK FOR IN PRAYER, BELIEVE THAT YOU HAVE RECEIVED IT, AND IT WILL BE YOURS."

MARK 11:24

SHANNON SEDGWICK DAVIS

USE YOUR GIFTS FOR GOOD

USE YOUR GIFTS FOR GOOD

Shannon Sedgwick Davis believes in the power of using her gifts. A partner at Bridgeway Foundation, the charitable giving arm of Bridgeway Capital Management in San Antonio, Texas, Shannon has embraced opportunities and affected lives by making the choice to use her innate talents and skills right where justice is needed. Having worked with International Justice Mission, serving on the advisory board for The Elders, a collective group of world leaders assembled to work on worldwide problems, and being on the board for multiple nonprofit organizations, like TOMS Shoes and Humanity United, Shannon has certainly made a mark on the world by using her gifts in service for those who need a voice.

Shannon is an attorney and an honors graduate of McMurry University and Baylor Law School. She received her graduate law degree in 2000, and instead of entering the lucrative world of corporate law, Shannon chose to make a mark by using her degree to help those who had suffered injustices but had no access to law professionals. There is value, she says, in the role that formal education can play in your desire to make a mark. "It is significant to distinguish yourself," she says, "by having a degree in your line of gifting." Is a college degree required to make a mark? No, but know what you were created to do. "We are each uniquely made to address a real need in the world," Shannon says. "Education can help you find that."

USE YOUR GIFTS FOR GOOD CONTINUED ON NEXT PAGE

SHANNON SEDGWICK DAVIS

USE YOUR GIFTS FOR GOOD CONTINUED

For the last three years, the majority of Shannon's work has focused on eradicating the Lord's Resistance Army (LRA) from its reign of terror in central Africa. Shannon has moved beyond advocacy and into action, traveling weeks at a time throughout 2012 to the areas of Africa that are affected by this militant group. It's not just about reconnaissance missions to rid the area of dangerous armies; for Shannon, she believes in knowing the people of the region and using that knowledge to determine how to help communities devastated by the LRA. "We get to know the people and hear their stories," she explains, "and then we come up with creative solutions alongside members of the communities. We also help with funding and implementation."

Along with making a mark in the world, Shannon believes in making a mark at home—raising two sons with her husband, talking with her boys about her calling and work, being involved in their schools. She uses her talents at home as well as around the globe. That's how she makes her mark.

WHAT'S YOUR MARK?

WHAT ARE YOUR UNIQUE TALENTS? WHAT ARE YOU SKILLED AT? HOW CAN YOU USE THOSE GIFTS TO MAKE A MARK?

These girls — beautiful, radiant, joyful, smiling — are some of those who have survived attacks by the LRA.

"'LOVE THE LORD YOUR GOD WITH ALL YOUR HEART AND WITH ALL YOUR SOUL AND WITH ALL YOUR MIND AND WITH ALL YOUR STRENGTH.' THE SECOND IS THIS: 'LOVE YOUR NEIGHBOR AS YOURSELF.' THERE IS NO COMMANDMENT GREATER THAN THESE."

MARK 12:30-31

⁹Those who went ahead and those who followed shouted,

"Hosanna!ᵃ"

"Blessed is he who comes in the name of the Lord!"ᵇ

¹⁰"Blessed is the coming kingdom of our father David!"

"Hosanna in the highest heaven!"

¹¹Jesus entered Jerusalem and went into the temple courts. He looked around at everything, but since it was already late, he went out to Bethany with the Twelve.

Jesus Curses a Fig Tree and Clears the Temple Courts

¹²The next day as they were leaving Bethany, Jesus was hungry. ¹³Seeing in the distance a fig tree in leaf, he went to find out if it had any fruit. When he reached it, he found nothing but leaves, because it was not the season for figs. ¹⁴Then he said to the tree, "May no one ever eat fruit from you again." And his disciples heard him say it.

¹⁵On reaching Jerusalem, Jesus entered the temple courts and began driving out those who were buying and selling there. He overturned the tables of the money changers and the benches of those selling doves, ¹⁶and would not allow anyone to carry merchandise through the temple courts. ¹⁷And as he taught them, he said, "Is it not written: 'My house will be called a house of prayer for all nations'ᶜ? But you have made it 'a den of robbers.'ᵈ"

¹⁸The chief priests and the teachers of the law heard this and began looking for a way to kill him, for they feared him, because the whole crowd was amazed at his teaching.

¹⁹When evening came, Jesus and his disciplesᵉ went out of the city.

²⁰In the morning, as they went along, they saw the fig tree withered from the roots. ²¹Peter remembered and said to Jesus, "Rabbi, look! The fig tree you cursed has withered!"

²²"Have faith in God," Jesus answered. ²³"Trulyᶠ I tell you, if anyone says to this mountain, 'Go, throw yourself into the sea,' and does not doubt in their heart but believes that what they say will happen, it will be done for them. ²⁴Therefore I tell you, whatever you ask for in prayer, believe that you have received it, and it will be yours. ²⁵And when you stand praying, if you hold anything against anyone, forgive them, so that your Father in heaven may forgive you your sins." [26]ᵍ

The Authority of Jesus Questioned

²⁷They arrived again in Jerusalem, and while Jesus was walking in the temple courts, the chief priests, the teachers of the law and the elders came to him. ²⁸"By what authority are you doing these things?" they asked. "And who gave you authority to do this?"

²⁹Jesus replied, "I will ask you one question. Answer me, and I will tell you by what authority I am doing these things. ³⁰John's baptism—was it from heaven, or of human origin? Tell me!"

³¹They discussed it among themselves and said, "If we say, 'From heaven,' he will ask, 'Then why didn't you believe him?' ³²But if we say, 'Of human origin' . . ." (They feared the people, for everyone held that John really was a prophet.)

³³So they answered Jesus, "We don't know."

Jesus said, "Neither will I tell you by what authority I am doing these things."

> Instead of looking for heroes, be one and help other people shine.
>
> **DONALD COLLINS**

The Parable of the Tenants

12 Jesus then began to speak to them in parables: "A man planted a vineyard. He put a wall around it, dug a pit for the winepress and built a watchtower. Then he rented the vineyard to some farmers and moved to another place. [2]At harvest time he sent a servant to the tenants to collect from them some of the fruit of the vineyard. [3]But they seized him, beat him and sent him away empty-handed. [4]Then he sent another servant to them; they struck this man on the head and treated him shamefully. [5]He sent still another, and that one they killed. He sent many others; some of them they beat, others they killed.

[6]"He had one left to send, a son, whom he loved. He sent him last of all, saying, 'They will respect my son.'

[7]"But the tenants said to one another, 'This is the heir. Come, let's kill him, and the inheritance will be ours.' [8]So they took him and killed him, and threw him out of the vineyard.

[9]"What then will the owner of the vineyard do? He will come and kill those tenants and give the vineyard to others. [10]Haven't you read this passage of Scripture:

"'The stone the builders rejected
    has become the cornerstone;
[11]the Lord has done this,
    and it is marvelous in our eyes'[a]?"

[12]Then the chief priests, the teachers of the law and the elders looked for a way to arrest him because they knew he had spoken the parable against them. But they were afraid of the crowd; so they left him and went away.

Paying the Imperial Tax to Caesar

[13]Later they sent some of the Pharisees and Herodians to Jesus to catch him in his words. [14]They came to him and said, "Teacher, we know that you are a man of integrity. You aren't swayed by others, because you pay no attention to who they are; but you teach the way of God in accordance with the truth. Is it right to pay the imperial tax[b] to Caesar or not? [15]Should we pay or shouldn't we?"

But Jesus knew their hypocrisy. "Why are you trying to trap me?" he asked. "Bring me a denarius and let me look at it." [16]They brought the coin, and he asked them, "Whose image is this? And whose inscription?"

"Caesar's," they replied.

[17]Then Jesus said to them, "Give back to Caesar what is Caesar's and to God what is God's."

And they were amazed at him.

Marriage at the Resurrection

[18]Then the Sadducees, who say there is no resurrection, came to him with a question. [19]"Teacher," they said, "Moses wrote for us that if a man's brother dies and leaves a wife but no children, the man must marry the widow and raise up offspring for his brother. [20]Now there were seven brothers. The first one married and died without leaving any children. [21]The second one married the widow, but he also died, leaving no child. It was the same with the third. [22]In fact, none of the seven left any children. Last of all, the woman died too. [23]At the resurrection[c] whose wife will she be, since the seven were married to her?"

[24]Jesus replied, "Are you not in error because you do not know the Scriptures or the power of God?

> We are each uniquely made to address a real need in the world.
>
> **SHANNON SEDGWICK DAVIS**

ANN VOSKAMP

THE SIMPLE THINGS

ANN VOSKAMP
THE SIMPLE THINGS

Ann Voskamp sits quietly at her home on a farm in Canada, writing away and changing lives at every turn. Ann is a farmer's wife, a mom of six and has been named by *Christianity Today* as one of the 50 leading women changing church and culture today. Deeply interested in helping the disadvantaged, she is a global advocate for the poor, traveling for Compassion International throughout Central America.

Having sold over half a million copies of her first book, *One Thousand Gifts: A Dare to Live Fully Right Where You Are,* Ann and her family seek ways to become the gift back. Partnering with Compassion, she was thrilled over the construction of an educational, vocational and recreational center for hundreds of children who live in the Guatemala City dump.

Ann's ability to leave a mark really centers on her heart for finding joy in the simple everyday moments. "This is a wondrous thing: We all make a mark. We can either mark the world or mar the world. It behooves us to leave a trail behind that leads to the better—greater life, deeper joy, more Truth. And who can disdain the small? It's the smallest strokes that add up to the greatest masterpieces."

Ann is content to be one of those small brushes, though her influence and voice are painting wider strokes every day. Her book was on the New York Times best-seller list for over a year, and her daily blog, AHolyExperience.com, is read by thousands every day. Ann is clearly living in such a way that her mark will not soon be forgotten.

THE SIMPLE THINGS CONTINUED ON NEXT PAGE

ANN VOSKAMP
THE SIMPLE THINGS CONTINUED

But she points away from herself at every opportunity, reminding us that it is Christ's move toward us first that makes even the simplest marks by us here on Earth even possible. "Christ didn't leave this world until he showed us his scars," she says, "and we won't leave this world until we leave our marks. To show him. In so many ways we need to leave a small footprint on the world—and a large heart print."

The simplest thing to remember is that everything we have is a gift. "A gift never stops being a gift. A gift is always meant to be given. It's a humbling and holy thing to influence others to pass on their gifts—their talents, their resources, their legacy."

"Pick up a pen and write down a thousand ways you've been blessed, a thousand gifts. It's all about coming to the startling realization that unlocks the deep places: I am blessed. I can bless. So this is happiness. Because the thing is, it's only when you know how much you've ridiculously received grace that you start to ridiculously extend grace."

WHAT'S YOUR MARK?

WHAT IS A SIMPLE WAY THAT YOU CAN MAKE A MARK TODAY?

Ann and her family sponsor Xiomara through Compassion International. They also partnered with Compassion to build an educational, vocational and recreational facility in Guatemala City to serve amazing children like Xiomara and the families who live in the Guatemala City dump. **Photo credit: "Ann Voskamp Guatemala Blog Trip" by Keely Marie Scott for © Compassion International**

BUT A POOR WIDOW
CAME AND PUT IN TWO
VERY SMALL COPPER
COINS, WORTH ONLY A
FEW CENTS. CALLING HIS
DISCIPLES TO HIM,
JESUS SAID, "TRULY I TELL
YOU, THIS POOR WIDOW
HAS PUT MORE INTO THE
TREASURY THAN ALL
THE OTHERS."

MARK 12:42-43

[25] When the dead rise, they will neither marry nor be given in marriage; they will be like the angels in heaven. [26] Now about the dead rising—have you not read in the Book of Moses, in the account of the burning bush, how God said to him, 'I am the God of Abraham, the God of Isaac, and the God of Jacob'*d*? [27] He is not the God of the dead, but of the living. You are badly mistaken!"

The Greatest Commandment

[28] One of the teachers of the law came and heard them debating. Noticing that Jesus had given them a good answer, he asked him, "Of all the commandments, which is the most important?"

[29] "The most important one," answered Jesus, "is this: 'Hear, O Israel: The Lord our God, the Lord is one.*e* [30] Love the Lord your God with all your heart and with all your soul and with all your mind and with all your strength.'*f* [31] The second is this: 'Love your neighbor as yourself.'*g* There is no commandment greater than these."

[32] "Well said, teacher," the man replied. "You are right in saying that God is one and there is no other but him. [33] To love him with all your heart, with all your understanding and with all your strength, and to love your neighbor as yourself is more important than all burnt offerings and sacrifices."

[34] When Jesus saw that he had answered wisely, he said to him, "You are not far from the kingdom of God." And from then on no one dared ask him any more questions.

Whose Son Is the Messiah?

[35] While Jesus was teaching in the temple courts, he asked, "Why do the teachers of the law say that the Messiah is the son of David? [36] David himself, speaking by the Holy Spirit, declared:

> "'The Lord said to my Lord:
>   "Sit at my right hand
> until I put your enemies
>   under your feet."'*b*

[37] David himself calls him 'Lord.' How then can he be his son?"

The large crowd listened to him with delight.

> We all make a mark. We can either mark the world or mar the world. It behooves us to leave a trail behind that leads to the better—greater life.
>
> **ANN VOSKAMP**

Warning Against the Teachers of the Law

[38] As he taught, Jesus said, "Watch out for the teachers of the law. They like to walk around in flowing robes and be greeted with respect in the marketplaces, [39] and have the most important seats in the synagogues and the places of honor at banquets. [40] They devour widows' houses and for a show make lengthy prayers. These men will be punished most severely."

The Widow's Offering

[41] Jesus sat down opposite the place where the offerings were put and watched the crowd putting their money into the temple treasury. Many rich people threw in large amounts. [42] But a poor widow came and put in two very small copper coins, worth only a few cents.

[43] Calling his disciples to him, Jesus said, "Truly I tell you, this poor widow has put more into the treasury than all the others. [44] They all gave out of their wealth; but she, out of her poverty, put in everything—all she had to live on."

The Destruction of the Temple and Signs of the End Times

13 As Jesus was leaving the temple, one of his disciples said to him, "Look, Teacher! What massive stones! What magnificent buildings!"

² "Do you see all these great buildings?" replied Jesus. "Not one stone here will be left on another; every one will be thrown down."

³ As Jesus was sitting on the Mount of Olives opposite the temple, Peter, James, John and Andrew asked him privately, ⁴ "Tell us, when will these things happen? And what will be the sign that they are all about to be fulfilled?"

⁵ Jesus said to them: "Watch out that no one deceives you. ⁶ Many will come in my name, claiming, 'I am he,' and will deceive many. ⁷ When you hear of wars and rumors of wars, do not be alarmed. Such things must happen, but the end is still to come. ⁸ Nation will rise against nation, and kingdom against kingdom. There will be earthquakes in various places, and famines. These are the beginning of birth pains.

⁹ "You must be on your guard. You will be handed over to the local councils and flogged in the synagogues. On account of me you will stand before governors and kings as witnesses to them. ¹⁰ And the gospel must first be preached to all nations. ¹¹ Whenever you are arrested and brought to trial, do not worry beforehand about what to say. Just say whatever is given you at the time, for it is not you speaking, but the Holy Spirit.

¹² "Brother will betray brother to death, and a father his child. Children will rebel against their parents and have them put to death. ¹³ Everyone will hate you because of me, but the one who stands firm to the end will be saved.

¹⁴ "When you see 'the abomination that causes desolation'ᵃ standing where itᵇ does not belong—let the reader understand—then let those who are in Judea flee to the mountains. ¹⁵ Let no one on the housetop go down or enter the house to take anything out. ¹⁶ Let no one in the field go back to get their cloak. ¹⁷ How dreadful it will be in those days for pregnant women and nursing mothers! ¹⁸ Pray that this will not take place in winter, ¹⁹ because those will be days of distress unequaled from the beginning, when God created the world, until now—and never to be equaled again.

²⁰ "If the Lord had not cut short those days, no one would survive. But for the sake of the elect, whom he has chosen, he has shortened them. ²¹ At that time if anyone says to you, 'Look, here is the Messiah!' or, 'Look, there he is!' do not believe it. ²² For false messiahs and false prophets will appear and perform signs and wonders to deceive, if possible, even the elect. ²³ So be on your guard; I have told you everything ahead of time.

²⁴ "But in those days, following that distress,

" 'the sun will be darkened,
    and the moon will not give its light;
²⁵ the stars will fall from the sky,
    and the heavenly bodies will be shaken.'ᶜ

²⁶ "At that time people will see the Son of Man coming in clouds with great power and glory. ²⁷ And he will send his angels and gather his elect from the four winds, from the ends of the earth to the ends of the heavens.

> Be aware of what humans need and what our hearts are craving.
>
> **CAITLIN CROSBY**

CAITLIN CROSBY
THE GIVING KEYS

CAITLIN CROSBY
THE GIVING KEYS

The truth is we need to only open our eyes to make a mark. Caitlin Crosby, actress, singer, songwriter and accidental entrepreneur, has found that her greatest impact has resulted from what she was able to see. As a singer/songwriter, Caitlin is known for her powerful lyrics, calming voice and commanding presence. She has a steadily growing fan base around the globe, and her acting career is equally established, with roles on *That 70s Show*, *Malcolm in the Middle* and MTV's *The Hard Times of RJ Berger.*

In addition to her career in entertainment, her time, her heart and her energy are also directed to what she sees on a daily basis: people in need—from the very rich to the very poor, in bank account or in spirit. "There is always a beautiful story to be told," she says. And she sees the beautiful stories waiting to be told, the ones that others overlook.

It began with Caitlin's encounters with young men and young women struggling with their imperfections. As Caitlin spoke with them, at shows or in small groups at church, she realized that their outlook was all wrong. "I wanted them to see that their flaws made them unique, not ugly." Caitlin, with Brie Larson, then created www.loveyourflawz.com, to allow people a place to celebrate their whole selves. She saw a hurt, a place where many struggled, and she filled it with a community-based website that continues to grow every day.

THE GIVING KEYS CONTINUED ON NEXT PAGE

CAITLIN CROSBY
THE GIVING KEYS CONTINUED

Caitlin next created The Giving Keys, a jewelry line that employs those trying to transition out of homelessness. Homeless people, those who are passed over daily, work at this business and in turn find purpose, employable skills, income and steps toward leaving homelessness behind. Each key necklace has a word imprinted on it. You wear it and then you give it away. "Once you 'pay it forward' to someone you feel needs the word/message on there, you then go back to TheGivingKeys.com website and write the story of why you gave it away." And the cycle continues as the stories inspire. With dreams to expand the jewelry line to other products, Caitlin is demonstrating to others how to share what they have and to see those right in front of them. It's more than paying it forward, it's giving away what you have, just like Jesus did.

Caitlin is learning as she goes. There is no formula, she says, to making a mark. "Be aware of what humans need and what our hearts are craving." And when she looks at the world like that, she finds that we are all on the same playing field. We are all in need. We are all beautiful stories waiting to be seen and be told.

WHAT'S YOUR MARK?

WHO DO YOU SEE WHO NEEDS HELP?

The Giving Keys is making a way for people struggling with homelessness to provide for themselves while giving hope, and beautiful jewelry, to many others.

"AND THE GOSPEL MUST FIRST BE PREACHED TO ALL NATIONS."

MARK 13:10

[28] "Now learn this lesson from the fig tree: As soon as its twigs get tender and its leaves come out, you know that summer is near. [29] Even so, when you see these things happening, you know that it[d] is near, right at the door. [30] Truly I tell you, this generation will certainly not pass away until all these things have happened. [31] Heaven and earth will pass away, but my words will never pass away.

The Day and Hour Unknown

[32] "But about that day or hour no one knows, not even the angels in heaven, nor the Son, but only the Father. [33] Be on guard! Be alert[e]! You do not know when that time will come. [34] It's like a man going away: He leaves his house and puts his servants in charge, each with their assigned task, and tells the one at the door to keep watch.

[35] "Therefore keep watch because you do not know when the owner of the house will come back—whether in the evening, or at midnight, or when the rooster crows, or at dawn. [36] If he comes suddenly, do not let him find you sleeping. [37] What I say to you, I say to everyone: 'Watch!' "

Jesus Anointed at Bethany

14 Now the Passover and the Festival of Unleavened Bread were only two days away, and the chief priests and the teachers of the law were scheming to arrest Jesus secretly and kill him. [2] "But not during the festival," they said, "or the people may riot."

[3] While he was in Bethany, reclining at the table in the home of Simon the Leper, a woman came with an alabaster jar of very expensive perfume, made of pure nard. She broke the jar and poured the perfume on his head.

[4] Some of those present were saying indignantly to one another, "Why this waste of perfume? [5] It could have been sold for more than a year's wages[a]

and the money given to the poor." And they rebuked her harshly.

[6] "Leave her alone," said Jesus. "Why are you bothering her? She has done a beautiful thing to me. [7] The poor you will always have with you,[b] and you can help them any time you want. But you will not always have me. [8] She did what she could. She poured perfume on my body beforehand to prepare for my burial. [9] Truly I tell you, wherever the gospel is preached throughout the world, what she has done will also be told, in memory of her."

[10] Then Judas Iscariot, one of the Twelve, went to the chief priests to betray Jesus to them. [11] They were delighted to hear this and promised to give him money. So he watched for an opportunity to hand him over.

The Last Supper

[12] On the first day of the Festival of Unleavened Bread, when it was customary to sacrifice the Passover lamb, Jesus' disciples asked him, "Where do you want us to go and make preparations for you to eat the Passover?"

[13] So he sent two of his disciples, telling them, "Go into the city, and a man carrying a jar of water will meet you. Follow him. [14] Say to the owner of the house he enters, 'The Teacher asks: Where is my guest room, where I may eat the Passover with my disciples?' [15] He will show you a large room upstairs, furnished and ready. Make preparations for us there."

[16] The disciples left, went into the city and found things just as Jesus had told them. So they prepared the Passover.

[17] When evening came, Jesus arrived with the Twelve. [18] While they were reclining at the table eating, he said, "Truly I tell you, one of you will betray me—one who is eating with me."

[19] They were saddened, and one by one they said to him, "Surely you don't mean me?"

²⁰"It is one of the Twelve," he replied, "one who dips bread into the bowl with me. ²¹The Son of Man will go just as it is written about him. But woe to that man who betrays the Son of Man! It would be better for him if he had not been born."

²²While they were eating, Jesus took bread, and when he had given thanks, he broke it and gave it to his disciples, saying, "Take it; this is my body."

²³Then he took a cup, and when he had given thanks, he gave it to them, and they all drank from it.

²⁴"This is my blood of the' covenant, which is poured out for many," he said to them. ²⁵"Truly I tell you, I will not drink again from the fruit of the vine until that day when I drink it new in the kingdom of God."

²⁶When they had sung a hymn, they went out to the Mount of Olives.

Jesus Predicts Peter's Denial

²⁷"You will all fall away," Jesus told them, "for it is written:

"'I will strike the shepherd,
   and the sheep will be
     scattered.'^d

²⁸But after I have risen, I will go ahead of you into Galilee."

²⁹Peter declared, "Even if all fall away, I will not."

³⁰"Truly I tell you," Jesus answered, "today—yes, tonight—before the rooster crows twice^e you yourself will disown me three times."

³¹But Peter insisted emphatically, "Even if I have to die with you, I will never disown you." And all the others said the same.

Gethsemane

³²They went to a place called Gethsemane, and Jesus said to his disciples, "Sit here while I pray." ³³He took Peter, James and John along with him, and he began to be deeply distressed and troubled. ³⁴"My soul is overwhelmed with sorrow to the point of death," he said to them. "Stay here and keep watch."

³⁵Going a little farther, he fell to the ground and prayed that if possible the hour might pass from him. ³⁶"*Abba*,^f Father," he said, "everything is possible for you. Take this cup from me. Yet not what I will, but what you will."

³⁷Then he returned to his disciples and found them sleeping. "Simon," he said to Peter, "are you asleep? Couldn't you keep watch for one hour? ³⁸Watch and pray so that you will not fall into temptation. The spirit is willing, but the flesh is weak."

³⁹Once more he went away and prayed the same thing. ⁴⁰When he came back, he again found them sleeping, because their eyes were heavy. They did not know what to say to him.

⁴¹Returning the third time, he said to them, "Are you still sleeping and resting? Enough! The hour has come. Look, the Son of Man is delivered into the hands of sinners. ⁴²Rise! Let us go! Here comes my betrayer!"

Jesus Arrested

⁴³Just as he was speaking, Judas, one of the Twelve, appeared. With him was a crowd armed with swords and clubs, sent from the chief priests, the teachers of the law, and the elders. ⁴⁴Now the betrayer had arranged a signal with them: "The one I kiss is the man; arrest him and lead him away under guard." ⁴⁵Going at once to Jesus, Judas said, "Rabbi!" and kissed him. ⁴⁶The men seized

> It's the tiny moments of saying yes that make for an extraordinary life.
>
> **KATIE DAVIS**

KATIE DAVIS

MODELING

KATIE DAVIS

MODELING

Katie Davis is not your average 20-something gal from Brentwood, Tennessee. A missionary, a foster mother of 13 Ugandan girls, the director of Amazima Ministries, author and blogger, Katie makes her mark on a daily basis in ways she never dreamed she would. She models a life lived for Christ in front of her children, as well as before her staff and community, each and every day. And over the years Katie has seen transformation around her as she has been transformed herself.

Kisses from Katie, her autobiography released in 2011, describes Katie's story of sacrifice and serving, leaving her home in Tennessee for a life in Uganda. The book, though, wasn't meant to spur others to leave their homes and relocate to Africa. Instead, Katie wants to inspire people to choose to say yes to the thing God has put in them.

Named Beliefnet's 2011 Most Inspirational Person of the Year, Katie's humble demeanor and quiet spirit shy away from praise. She had one goal when she set out for Africa: to love well. "I honestly never meant to make a mark on the US side—the readers of the blog and the book—I just meant to make a mark in Uganda." And it seems that as she has set her focus there, the world has been touched, changed, by her life.

An unexpected impact? The change in her community. Katie started Amazima Ministries to care for the orphaned children in her area who have relatives who can care for them but not enough funds for them to take on another child. Through donations from supporters around the world, Amazima is able to provide medical care, food and schooling to 600 children who are able to live with someone in their biological family. For the children who have no living relatives, Katie has watched as twelve

MODELING CONTINUED ON NEXT PAGE

KATIE DAVIS
MODELING CONTINUED

families in the community, including four staff members, have stepped up and adopted foster children from within their own towns.

Katie models a love that isn't defined by biological birth, and as she has made that kind of mark, lived that kind of life, others have been marked and changed, and futures are different because of her.

"People look at my life," she says, "and they think they could never have 13 adopted children and run a nonprofit organization. Truth is, this has grown so much. I couldn't have planned this or known I could do this either! I just started saying yes to the little things." And each little yes that Katie has whispered with her life, every open door she has stepped through, has made a way for her to not only keep walking but to blaze a trail for those behind her. "It's the tiny moments of saying yes that make for an extraordinary life," Katie says, and she does that. She models that. Her mark is widespread, and the world is different because of her.

▶ WHAT'S YOUR MARK? ◀

HOW IS YOUR MARK AFFECTING OTHERS IN YOUR COMMUNITY?

Katie loves spending time with the thirteen Ugandan girls she fosters and is in the process of adopting.
Photo credit: "Katie's Fun Family Feet 88" by Jacqueline Grace Kramlich

"I AM," SAID JESUS.

"AND YOU WILL SEE THE SON OF MAN SITTING AT THE RIGHT HAND OF THE MIGHTY ONE AND COMING ON THE CLOUDS OF HEAVEN."

MARK 14:62

Jesus and arrested him. ⁴⁷Then one of those standing near drew his sword and struck the servant of the high priest, cutting off his ear.

⁴⁸"Am I leading a rebellion," said Jesus, "that you have come out with swords and clubs to capture me? ⁴⁹Every day I was with you, teaching in the temple courts, and you did not arrest me. But the Scriptures must be fulfilled." ⁵⁰Then everyone deserted him and fled.

⁵¹A young man, wearing nothing but a linen garment, was following Jesus. When they seized him, ⁵²he fled naked, leaving his garment behind.

Jesus Before the Sanhedrin

⁵³They took Jesus to the high priest, and all the chief priests, the elders and the teachers of the law came together. ⁵⁴Peter followed him at a distance, right into the courtyard of the high priest. There he sat with the guards and warmed himself at the fire.

⁵⁵The chief priests and the whole Sanhedrin were looking for evidence against Jesus so that they could put him to death, but they did not find any. ⁵⁶Many testified falsely against him, but their statements did not agree.

⁵⁷Then some stood up and gave this false testimony against him: ⁵⁸"We heard him say, 'I will destroy this temple made with human hands and in three days will build another, not made with hands.' " ⁵⁹Yet even then their testimony did not agree.

⁶⁰Then the high priest stood up before them and asked Jesus, "Are you not going to answer? What is this testimony that these men are bringing against you?" ⁶¹But Jesus remained silent and gave no answer.

Again the high priest asked him, "Are you the Messiah, the Son of the Blessed One?"

⁶²"I am," said Jesus. "And you will see the Son of Man sitting at the right hand of the Mighty One and coming on the clouds of heaven."

⁶³The high priest tore his clothes. "Why do we need any more witnesses?" he asked. ⁶⁴"You have heard the blasphemy. What do you think?"

They all condemned him as worthy of death. ⁶⁵Then some began to spit at him; they blindfolded him, struck him with their fists, and said, "Prophesy!" And the guards took him and beat him.

Peter Disowns Jesus

⁶⁶While Peter was below in the courtyard, one of the servant girls of the high priest came by. ⁶⁷When she saw Peter warming himself, she looked closely at him.

"You also were with that Nazarene, Jesus," she said.

⁶⁸But he denied it. "I don't know or understand what you're talking about," he said, and went out into the entryway.ᵍ

⁶⁹When the servant girl saw him there, she said again to those standing around, "This fellow is one of them." ⁷⁰Again he denied it.

After a little while, those standing near said to Peter, "Surely you are one of them, for you are a Galilean."

⁷¹He began to call down curses, and he swore to them, "I don't know this man you're talking about."

⁷²Immediately the rooster crowed the second time.ʰ Then Peter remembered the word Jesus had spoken to him: "Before the rooster crows twiceⁱ you will disown me three times." And he broke down and wept.

Jesus Before Pilate

15 Very early in the morning, the chief priests, with the elders, the teachers of the law and the whole Sanhedrin, made their plans. So they bound Jesus, led him away and handed him over to Pilate.

²"Are you the king of the Jews?" asked Pilate.

"You have said so," Jesus replied.

[3] The chief priests accused him of many things. [4] So again Pilate asked him, "Aren't you going to answer? See how many things they are accusing you of."

[5] But Jesus still made no reply, and Pilate was amazed.

[6] Now it was the custom at the festival to release a prisoner whom the people requested. [7] A man called Barabbas was in prison with the insurrectionists who had committed murder in the uprising. [8] The crowd came up and asked Pilate to do for them what he usually did.

[9] "Do you want me to release to you the king of the Jews?" asked Pilate, [10] knowing it was out of self-interest that the chief priests had handed Jesus over to him. [11] But the chief priests stirred up the crowd to have Pilate release Barabbas instead.

[12] "What shall I do, then, with the one you call the king of the Jews?" Pilate asked them.

[13] "Crucify him!" they shouted.

[14] "Why? What crime has he committed?" asked Pilate.

But they shouted all the louder, "Crucify him!"

[15] Wanting to satisfy the crowd, Pilate released Barabbas to them. He had Jesus flogged, and handed him over to be crucified.

The Soldiers Mock Jesus

[16] The soldiers led Jesus away into the palace (that is, the Praetorium) and called together the whole company of soldiers. [17] They put a purple robe on him, then twisted together a crown of thorns and set it on him. [18] And they began to call out to him, "Hail, king of the Jews!" [19] Again and again they struck him on the head with a staff and spit on him. Falling on their knees, they paid homage to him. [20] And when they had mocked him, they took off the purple robe and put his own clothes on him. Then they led him out to crucify him.

The Crucifixion of Jesus

[21] A certain man from Cyrene, Simon, the father of Alexander and Rufus, was passing by on his way in from the country, and they forced him to carry the cross. [22] They brought Jesus to the place called Golgotha (which means "the place of the skull"). [23] Then they offered him wine mixed with myrrh, but he did not take it. [24] And they crucified him. Dividing up his clothes, they cast lots to see what each would get.

[25] It was nine in the morning when they crucified him. [26] The written notice of the charge against him read: THE KING OF THE JEWS.

[27] They crucified two rebels with him, one on his right and one on his left. [28]a [29] Those who passed by hurled insults at him, shaking their heads and saying, "So! You who are going to destroy the temple and build it in three days, [30] come down from the cross and save yourself!" [31] In the same way the chief priests and the teachers of the law mocked him among themselves. "He saved others," they said, "but he can't save himself! [32] Let this Messiah, this king of Israel, come down now from the cross, that we may see and believe." Those crucified with him also heaped insults on him.

The Death of Jesus

[33] At noon, darkness came over the whole land until three in the afternoon. [34] And at three in the

> As we become ... more available to loving our neighbor, we get more chances to do that.
>
> **BOB GOFF**

BOB GOFF

BE AVAILABLE

BOB GOFF
BE AVAILABLE

Bob Goff doesn't make appointments. He doesn't let a call go to voice mail. He doesn't seem to prioritize one human over another, except for his family. "They're like the center ring of the tree," Bob says. "Everything else grows out of that place."

Bob Goff is the New York Times best-selling author of *Love Does*, as well as an attorney who founded Restore International, a nonprofit human rights organization operating in Uganda and India. He also serves as the honorable consul for the Republic of Uganda to the United States.

Bob also throws parades with no spectators, only participants, works out of an office located at Disneyland and prints his cell phone number in the back of each copy of *Love Does*. But all of this is just part of being available, Bob says. "As we become more and more available to loving our neighbors, we get more chances to do that." The mark grows, the impact grows and hearts are changed.

Bob invests in people. He meets musicians and artists and invites them to a retreat at his home in Canada. He answers every call that comes to his phone, sometimes up to 40 a day. He has a crazy idea and gets others to buy into it. Throughout *Love Does*, he tells stories of his grand capers and his everyday capers and how he convinces others to get involved.

A well-respected construction lawyer long before he was an author and household name in many circles, Bob is a pioneer, a trailblazer. Restore International, begun in 2004, focuses on bringing to

BE AVAILABLE CONTINUED ON NEXT PAGE

BE AVAILABLE CONTINUED

justice those engaged in human trafficking, but it also works to help the victims through education and rehabilitation. Restore also works with judicial systems to improve human rights standards.

"I break trail, and then everyone is invited," Bob explains. And it is true. Whether it is the "anyone-is-welcome" trips to Uganda or the yearly parades, Bob's life is what he says. Make friends. Invite them to play along. Make a mark by being available to the people around you and those in need. "It's about availability, compassion, love—not about a person's title or status." Bob says that this is making a mark: focusing on the person, not the position, and finding the thing in your heart that feels like your next big caper.

"Go do your own thing," Bob says. "Be loving, and keep your eyes on Jesus."

WHAT'S YOUR MARK?

HOW CAN YOU MAKE A GREATER MARK BY BEING AVAILABLE?

This remand home in Masindi, Uganda, is now empty—these boys have been released after their cases were brought to trial.
Photo credit: "Masindi Jail Photos" by © Jay Milbrandt 2010

"DON'T BE ALARMED," HE SAID. "YOU ARE LOOKING FOR JESUS THE NAZARENE, WHO WAS CRUCIFIED. HE HAS RISEN! HE IS NOT HERE. SEE THE PLACE WHERE THEY LAID HIM."

MARK 16:6

afternoon Jesus cried out in a loud voice, "*Eloi, Eloi, lema sabachthani?*" (which means "My God, my God, why have you forsaken me?").[b]

[35] When some of those standing near heard this, they said, "Listen, he's calling Elijah."

[36] Someone ran, filled a sponge with wine vinegar, put it on a staff, and offered it to Jesus to drink. "Now leave him alone. Let's see if Elijah comes to take him down," he said.

[37] With a loud cry, Jesus breathed his last.

[38] The curtain of the temple was torn in two from top to bottom. [39] And when the centurion, who stood there in front of Jesus, saw how he died,[c] he said, "Surely this man was the Son of God!"

[40] Some women were watching from a distance. Among them were Mary Magdalene, Mary the mother of James the younger and of Joseph,[d] and Salome. [41] In Galilee these women had followed him and cared for his needs. Many other women who had come up with him to Jerusalem were also there.

The Burial of Jesus

[42] It was Preparation Day (that is, the day before the Sabbath). So as evening approached, [43] Joseph of Arimathea, a prominent member of the Council, who was himself waiting for the kingdom of God, went boldly to Pilate and asked for Jesus' body. [44] Pilate was surprised to hear that he was already dead. Summoning the centurion, he asked him if Jesus had already died. [45] When he learned from the centurion that it was so, he gave the body to Joseph. [46] So Joseph bought some linen cloth, took down the body, wrapped it in the linen, and placed it in a tomb cut out of rock. Then he rolled a stone against the entrance of the tomb. [47] Mary Magdalene and Mary the mother of Joseph saw where he was laid.

Jesus Has Risen

16 When the Sabbath was over, Mary Magdalene, Mary the mother of James, and Salome bought spices so that they might go to anoint Jesus' body. [2] Very early on the first day of the week, just after sunrise, they were on their way to the tomb [3] and they asked each other, "Who will roll the stone away from the entrance of the tomb?"

[4] But when they looked up, they saw that the stone, which was very large, had been rolled away. [5] As they entered the tomb, they saw a young man dressed in a white robe sitting on the right side, and they were alarmed.

[6] "Don't be alarmed," he said. "You are looking for Jesus the Nazarene, who was crucified. He has risen! He is not here. See the place where they laid him. [7] But go, tell his disciples and Peter, 'He is going ahead of you into Galilee. There you will see him, just as he told you.'"

[8] Trembling and bewildered, the women went out and fled from the tomb. They said nothing to anyone, because they were afraid.[a]

> Go into all the world and preach the gospel to all creation.
>
> **JESUS**

[The earliest manuscripts and some other ancient witnesses do not have verses 9–20.]

[9] *When Jesus rose early on the first day of the week, he appeared first to Mary Magdalene, out of whom he had driven seven demons.* [10] *She went and told those who had been with him and*

who were mourning and weeping. [11] When they heard that Jesus was alive and that she had seen him, they did not believe it.

[12] Afterward Jesus appeared in a different form to two of them while they were walking in the country. [13] These returned and reported it to the rest; but they did not believe them either.

[14] Later Jesus appeared to the Eleven as they were eating; he rebuked them for their lack of faith and their stubborn refusal to believe those who had seen him after he had risen.

[15] He said to them, "Go into all the world and preach the gospel to all creation. [16] Whoever believes and is baptized will be saved, but whoever does not believe will be condemned. [17] And these signs will accompany those who believe: In my name they will drive out demons; they will speak in new tongues; [18] they will pick up snakes with their hands; and when they drink deadly poison, it will not hurt them at all; they will place their hands on sick people, and they will get well."

[19] After the Lord Jesus had spoken to them, he was taken up into heaven and he sat at the right hand of God. [20] Then the disciples went out and preached everywhere, and the Lord worked with them and confirmed his word by the signs that accompanied it.

End Notes

Chapter 1: [a] 1 Or Jesus Christ. Messiah (Hebrew) and Christ (Greek) both mean Anointed One.   [b] 1 Some manuscripts do not have the Son of God.   [c] 2 Mal. 3:1   [d] 3 Isaiah 40:3   [e] 8 Or in   [f] 13 The Greek for tempted can also mean tested.   [g] 40 The Greek word traditionally translated leprosy was used for various diseases affecting the skin.   [h] 41 Many manuscripts Jesus was filled with compassion   **Chapter 3:** [a] 14 Some manuscripts twelve—designating them apostles—   [b] 21 Or his associates   **Chapter 4:** [a] 12 Isaiah 6:9,10   **Chapter 5:** [a] 1 Some manuscripts Gadarenes; other manuscripts Gergesenes   [b] 20 That is, the Ten Cities   [c] 36 Or Ignoring   **Chapter 6:** [a] 3: Greek Joses, a variant of Joseph   [b] 14 Some early manuscripts He was saying   [c] 20 Some early manuscripts he did many things   [d] 22 Some early manuscripts When his daughter   [e] 37 Greek take two hundred denarii   **Chapter 7:** [a] 4 Some early manuscripts pitchers, kettles and dining couches   [b] 6,7 Isaiah 29:13   [c] 9 Some manuscripts set up   [d] 10 Exodus 20:12; Deut. 5:16   [e] 10 Exodus 21:17; Lev. 20:9   [f] 16 Some manuscripts include here the words of 4:23.   [g] 24 Many early manuscripts Tyre and Sidon   [h] 31 That is, the Ten Cities   **Chapter 8:** [a] 26 Some manuscripts go and tell anyone in   [b] 35 The Greek word means either life or soul; also in verses 36 and 37.   **Chapter 9:** [a] 29 Some manuscripts prayer and fasting   [b] 44 Some manuscripts include here the words of verse 48.   [c] 46 Some manuscripts include here the words of verse 48.   [d] 48 Isaiah 66:24   **Chapter 10:** [a] 6 Gen. 1:27   [b] 7 Some early manuscripts do not have and be united to his wife.   [c] 8 Gen. 2:24   [d] 19 Exodus 20:12-16; Deut. 5:16-20   [e] 24 Some manuscripts is for those who trust in riches   **Chapter 11:** [a] 9 A Hebrew expression meaning "Save!" which became an exclamation of praise; also in verse 10   [b] 9 Psalm 118:25,26   [c] 17 Isaiah 56:7   [d] 17 Jer. 7:11   [e] 19 Some early manuscripts came, Jesus   [f] 22,23 Some early manuscripts "If you have faith in God," Jesus answered, [23] "truly   [g] 26 Some manuscripts include here words similar to Matt. 6:15.   **Chapter 12:** [a] 11 Psalm 118:22,23   [b] 14 A special tax levied on subject peoples, not on Roman citizens   [c] 23 Some manuscripts resurrection, when people rise from the dead,   [d] 26 Exodus 3:6   [e] 29 Or The Lord our God is one Lord   [f] 30 Deut. 6:4,5   [g] 31 Lev. 19:18   [h] 36 Psalm 110:1   **Chapter 13:** [a] 14 Daniel 9:27; 11:31; 12:11   [b] 14 Or he   [c] 25 Isaiah 13:10; 34:4   [d] 29 Or he   [e] 33 Some manuscripts alert and pray   **Chapter 14:** [a] 5 Greek than three hundred denarii   [b] 7 See Deut. 15:11.   [c] 24 Some manuscripts the new   [d] 27 Zech. 13:7   [e] 30 Some early manuscripts do not have twice.   [f] 36 Aramaic for father   [g] 68 Some early manuscripts entryway and the rooster crowed   [h] 72 Some early manuscripts do not have the second time.   [i] 72 Some early manuscripts do not have twice.   **Chapter 15:** [a] 28 Some manuscripts include here words similar to Luke 22:37.   [b] 34 Psalm 22:1   [c] 39 Some manuscripts saw that he died with such a cry   [d] 40 Greek Joses, a variant of Joseph; also in verse 47   **Chapter 16:** [a] 8 Some manuscripts have the following ending between verses 8 and 9, and one manuscript has it after verse 8 (omitting verses 9-20): Then they quickly reported all these instructions to those around Peter. After this, Jesus himself also sent out through them from east to west the sacred and imperishable proclamation of eternal salvation. Amen.

MARK

FOLLOWER OF JESUS

Imagine sitting around a campfire and next to you sits Peter—fisherman, Jesus-follower, sinner and disciple. Peter is telling stories about the incredible adventures he shared with Jesus. Also at the campfire is John Mark. He listens closely, absorbing every word.

The Gospel of Mark is a gospel of exploits: short, to-the-point, action-oriented and focusing on Jesus' miracles. This Gospel came about as John Mark listened to Peter's stories and then recorded them so the rest of the world could sit next to Peter and hear of the wonders of following Jesus.

John Mark wasn't one of Jesus' disciples. He was a young relative of one of the founders of the Christian church, a man with the wonderful name of Barnabas (which means "son of encouragement"). Mark accompanied his cousin Barnabas and the great evangelist Paul on what is known as Paul's "first missionary journey." However, along the way John Mark left them and returned to Jerusalem (see Acts 13:13). As a result, Paul refused to take Mark with him on his second missionary journey. But Paul and Mark later reconciled and worked together in Rome. And in his own letter, Peter, who had known John Mark and his family for many years, affectionately refers to him as his "son" (see 1 Peter 5:13).

We don't know the details about Mark's failed first journey as a missionary, but his journey from disgrace to reinstatement in the greatest cause of all time gives us hope. We're all human—not one single one of us who does God's work is flawlessly perfect. Mark experienced failure, but his Gospel stands as a testament to God's ability to work through broken vessels. And as John Mark persevered, he made a mark on the world that endures to this day.

KNOWN FOR HIS
HEALING HANDS AND
COMPASSIONATE
HEART, JESUS CHRIST,
IN LIFE, DEATH, AND
RESURRECTION,
HAS MARKED THIS
PLANET.

JESUS

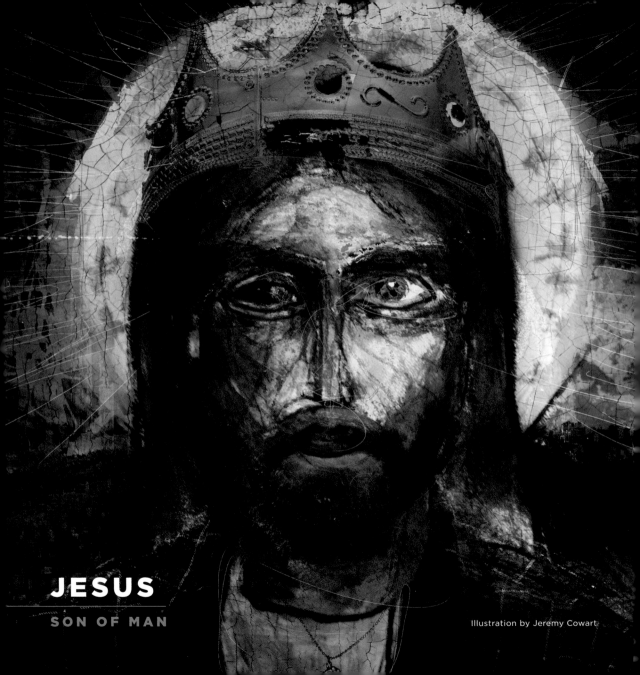

JESUS

SON OF MAN

Illustration by Jeremy Cowart

SON OF MAN

A little over 2,000 years ago, a mark-maker came into our world, and things have never been the same. Jesus Christ, son of God, made the humblest of entries to Earth and in that humbleness has marked all his followers to live generous and loving lives. Jesus isn't remembered for the impact he made in his workplace, though he followed in the footsteps of his father as a carpenter. It was not his art or his organization or his platform.

It was his actions. When he moved, when he prayed, when he healed, when he sacrificed, lives were changed. Marks were made. And as those around him watched and took part in the stories, they recorded them and made them available to us, thousands of years later, to read and study and digest. The Bible, fully true and God-breathed, is our glimpse into the changed lives that surrounded Jesus and were because of Jesus. "I am the way and the truth and the life," Jesus says, and millions of people through thousands of generations have believed him.

Known for his healing hands and compassionate heart, Jesus Christ, in life, death and resurrection, has marked this planet. He is the standard. He is the heart we want to have, the hands we want to mimic, the lifestyle we want to adopt. As the Moravian missionaries used to say, "may the Lamb receive the reward for his suffering." In death, Jesus suffered marks that changed the course of history, opened up doors long sealed, and freed souls for generations to come. His reward? Us, making our mark, changing the world on his behalf, loving the way he loved, serving the way he served.

MAKE YOUR MARK. HE IS OUR GREAT REWARD, AND WE ARE HIS.

WHAT'S YOUR MARK?

JEREMY COWART

MAKING HIS MARK WAS A CHOICE.

Jeremy Cowart is a professional photographer from Nashville, Tennessee. Beginning his photography career in 2005, Jeremy quickly became a respected artistic voice in the industry. Jeremy has had a wide range of photographic experiences, including high-end celebrity shoots, album covers, commercial advertisements, traveling on a world tour with Britney Spears and photographing events in seventeen countries with the Passion World Tour in 2008. Though all of these photography genres are different, the goal is still the same: to use the camera to create beautiful art and tell a new story.

Not only has Jeremy photographed some of the most famous faces in the world, he also uses his time and gifts to give back to those around him. Jeremy enjoys spending his time on social art, developing and working on creative, collaborative projects that will make an impact. Jeremy has worked with multiple nonprofit organizations and traveled throughout Africa and Haiti to photograph and bring awareness to the needs of those people. He is also the founder of Help-Portrait, a worldwide movement of photographers using their time, equipment and expertise to give back to those less fortunate.

CAMERON STRANG

TIM AND CINDY HOFFMAN

MIKE FOSTER

CATHERINE ROHR

KAREN BROWN

CHARLOTTE MOORE

JENNY CROSS

JEREMY BOUMA

JESUS MADE HIS MARK.
FOLLOW HIM.
IT'S TIME TO MAKE
YOUR MARK.
SHAREYOURMARK.COM